"David Helm has written the most helpful, concise, and useful book on expository preaching I have ever read."

Matt Chandler, Lead Pastor, The Village Church, Dallas, Texas; President, Acts 29 Church Planting Network

"If I were teaching a preaching class and could assign the students only one book, this might be the one. It's a rare find that both introduces a topic to the novice and instructs the experienced. David's humility convicts, rebukes, instructs, and encourages me as a preacher. I pray it will do the same for you."

Mark Dever, Senior Pastor, Capitol Hill Baptist Church, Washington, DC; President, 9Marks

"David Helm's skills as a preacher and his vast experience as a teacher of preachers make anything he says on this subject of great value. But I read him with greatest appreciation for what is most clear among his commitments: 'Staying on the line, never rising above the text of Scripture to say more than it said and never falling beneath the text by lessening its force or fullness.' Here is not merely skill and wisdom, but also faithfulness from which the truest treasures of preaching come."

Bryan Chapell, President Emeritus, Covenant Theological Seminary; Senior Pastor, Grace Presbyterian Church, Peoria, Illinois

"Helm has given us a finely wrought and utterly compelling brief on what needs to be understood and done in order to faithfully preach the Word. This is an important book."

R. Kent Hughes, Senior Pastor Emeritus, College Church, Wheaton, Illinois

"In this compact book, David Helm distills key principles and insights that have encouraged many at the Charles Simeon Trust preaching workshops. I have seen men reengage with the hard work of preaching preparation as David has taught this material. May that same result be multiplied by this book."

Paul Rees, Senior Pastor, Charlotte Chapel, Edinburgh, Scotland

"I love to see people's shocked responses when they learn that expository preaching is the first of the '9 Marks of a Healthy Church.' This priority is affirmed and explained in *Expositional Preaching*. David Helm issues a stirring challenge to get the message clear and right. May God be pleased to use this book to help you preach faithfully for the health of the church and the glory of God!"

H. B. Charles Jr., Pastor, Shiloh Metropolitan Baptist Church, Jacksonville, Florida

EXPOSITIONAL PREACHING

9Marks: Building Healthy Churches

Edited by Mark Dever and Jonathan Leeman

Expositional Preaching: How We Speak God's Word Today,
  David Helm

*Sound Doctrine: How a Church Grows in the Love and Holiness
  of God,* Bobby Jamieson

The Gospel: How the Church Portrays the Beauty of Christ,
  Ray Ortlund

Evangelism: How the Whole Church Speaks of Jesus,
  J. Mack Stiles

*Church Membership: How the World Knows Who Represents
  Jesus,* Jonathan Leeman

Church Discipline: How the Church Protects the Name of Jesus,
  Jonathan Leeman

Discipling: How to Help Others Follow Jesus, Mark Dever

Church Elders: How to Shepherd God's People Like Jesus,
  Jeramie Rinne

BUILDING HEALTHY CHURCHES

EXPOSITIONAL PREACHING

HOW
WE SPEAK
GOD'S WORD
TODAY

DAVID HELM

CROSSWAY®

WHEATON, ILLINOIS

Expositional Preaching: How We Speak God's Word Today

Copyright © 2014 by The Charles Simeon Trust

Published by Crossway
    1300 Crescent Street
    Wheaton, Illinois 60187

Cover design: Dual Identity, inc.

Cover image: Wayne Brezinka for brezinkadesign.com

First printing 2014

Printed in the United States of America

Hardcover ISBN: 978-1-4335-4313-5
ePub ISBN: 978-1-4335-4316-6
PDF ISBN: 978-1-4335-4314-2
Mobipocket ISBN: 978-1-4335-4315-9

Library of Congress Cataloging-in-Publication Data

Helm, David R., 1961–
 Expositional preaching : how we speak God's word today / David Helm.
  pages cm.—(9Marks: building healthy churches)
 Includes bibliographical references and index.
 ISBN 978-1-4335-4313-5 (hc)
 1. Expository preaching. I. Title.
BV4211.3.H46   2014
251—dc23   2013036437

Crossway is a publishing ministry of Good News Publishers.

LB		27	26	25	24	23	22	21	20	19	18
17	16	15	14	13	12	11	10	9	8	7	6

CONTENTS

SERIES PREFACE

Do you believe it's your responsibility to help build a healthy church? If you are a Christian, we believe that it is.

Jesus commands you to make disciples (Matt. 28:18–20). Jude says to build yourselves up in the faith (Jude 20–21). Peter calls you to use your gifts to serve others (1 Pet. 4:10). Paul tells you to speak the truth in love so that your church will become mature (Eph. 4:13, 15). Do you see where we are getting this?

Whether you are a church member or leader, the Building Healthy Churches series of books aims to help you fulfill such biblical commands and so play your part in building a healthy church. Another way to say it might be, we hope these books will help you grow in loving your church like Jesus loves your church.

9Marks plans to produce a short, readable book on each of what Mark has called nine marks of a healthy church, plus one more on sound doctrine. Watch for books on expositional preaching, biblical theology, the gospel, conversion, evangelism, church membership, church discipline, discipleship and growth, and church leadership.

Local churches exist to display God's glory to the nations. We do that by fixing our eyes on the gospel of Jesus Christ, trusting him for salvation, and then loving one another with

God's own holiness, unity, and love. We pray the book you are holding will help.

With hope,
Mark Dever and Jonathan Leeman
Series editors

INTRODUCTION

Old Bones

The great man's body rests in a vault beneath the stone floor of King's College Chapel in Cambridge, England, just inside the near west door. The site has two markings: "CS," and the year this man died, "1836." Both have been cut into the stone pavement and filled with lead. Should you ever get the chance to stand there—as I once did in awe—know this: the old bones beneath your feet belong to one who returned the Bible to the center of church life in England.

It was a sad November day in 1836 when no fewer than 1,500 gownsmen attended the funeral of Charles Simeon. In unprecedented numbers for the time, people came to pay their respects to this pastor and preacher.[1] Charles Simeon was a gift, God's gift, to the people of his generation.

He is a gift to our generation as well. His gospel instincts have stood the test of time and can make a fresh impression on preaching in our day. For Simeon's preaching had something that much of our preaching lacks.

What is it we lack? How can we benefit?

The answers are surprisingly simple and point us to the very heart of this thing called *expositional preaching*. In large measure, the great man's conviction about the Bible was the source of his influence. Simeon believed that a simple and clear explication of the Bible is what makes a church healthy and happy. Biblical exposition does the heavy lifting of building up a church. This abiding belief never left Simeon. For fifty-four years, and from a single pulpit in a university town, he tirelessly gave himself to the primacy of preaching. Week by week, year by year, and decade by decade he stood in the pulpit and declared God's Word with clarity, simplicity, and power. He defined his conviction about biblical exposition this way:

> My endeavor is to bring out of Scripture what is there, and not to thrust in what I think might be there. I have a great jealousy on this head; never to speak more or less than I believe to be the mind of the Spirit in the passage I am expounding.[2]

Simeon viewed the preacher as duty-bound to the text. He was committed to staying on the line, never rising above the text of Scripture to say more than it said and never falling beneath the text by lessening its force or fullness.

This conviction—this mature restraint—is often missed today by those who handle God's Word. Frankly, it is the undoing of so many of our churches, even doctrinally sound ones. Much of what we think is faithful biblical preaching actually misses the mark because of a lack of restraint. And let me be the first to admit that I have not always exercised the restraint of bringing out of Scripture only what is there. It is my prayer that this little book, among other things, might be used by God to help anyone explore the ways that teachers and preachers of the Bible might rediscover this conviction.

But it is not only Simeon's conviction that is worth considering. Simeon's goals in preaching need to be recovered. He tightly framed his aims for biblical exposition this way:

> to humble the sinner;
> to exalt the Saviour;
> to promote holiness.[3]

It doesn't get any clearer than that. And these aims should guide us today. Our world, like Simeon's, desperately needs to know how deep humanity has fallen, how high Jesus Christ has ascended, and what God requires of his people. The best and only way to help this world is to speak God's words in the power of the Spirit. How do we do this? What does it look like?

The answers are found in expositional preaching. Expositional preaching is empowered preaching that rightfully submits the shape and emphasis of the sermon to the shape and emphasis of a biblical text. In that way it brings out of the text what the Holy Spirit put there, as Simeon put it, and does not put into the text what the preacher thinks might be there. The process is a little more complex. That is what the rest of this book is about.

We will begin by thinking about the mistakes so many of us make, mistakes which particularly result from our attempts to contextualize. Then we will consider the challenges and demands of exegeting a text, understanding a text in light of the entire biblical canon, and then preaching it to our own context.

Though this book will serve adequately as an introduction to expositional preaching, one of my hopes is that the person who is already preaching or teaching the Bible will find that it offers a useful grid by which to examine what you are presently doing. It is almost meant as a "follow-up," a way of giving you the chance to ask yourself, "Okay, is this what I am doing? Am I bringing out of Scripture only what is there? Am I doing so in ways that rightly humble the listener, exalt the Savior, and promote holiness in the lives of those present?"

The demands and challenges of expositional preaching are many. And making progress in our ability to handle God's Word faithfully will not be easy. But I am certain of this: if preachers and church leaders today allow the simplicity of Simeon's conviction and aims to speak to us from the grave, the health and happiness of the church can be restored.

So let's get started.

1

CONTEXTUALIZATION

Contextualization is essential to good exposition. And the sermon manuscripts we have from St. Augustine lead some to suggest that he did it quite well.

> Thus when Augustine propounded ideas about society that were taken straight from the pagan classics, we should not think that he was doing this in a self-conscious effort to impress pagans with his culture or to woo them into the church by citing their favorite authors. He did it as unthinkingly as we, today, say that the earth is round. . . . He presented much of what he had to say . . . as a matter of common sense.[1]

I love what Augustine's attitude toward contextualization teaches us about its relationship to preaching. His surprising ability to connect to his listeners was the result of his general interest in life; it was not a calculated outcome brought about by harvesting cultural references in hopes of coming off as relevant. This chapter will address the problems that emerge when contextualization of the latter sort takes over the preacher when he is preparing his message.

In the introduction, we caught a small glimpse of what expositional preaching should be. It is an endeavor to bring out of Scripture what is there, to never thrust into a text what the Holy Spirit didn't put there, and to do so from a particular text in ways that rightly humble the listener, exalt the Savior, and promote holiness in the lives of those present. While we haven't yet described how a sermon should do all of this, it is worth taking time here to consider some common ways our preaching can miss the mark.

THE BLIND ADHERENCE PROBLEM

What do I mean by contextualization in preaching?[2] In simple terms, contextualization in preaching is communicating the gospel message in ways that are understandable or appropriate to the listener's cultural context. In other words, contextualization is concerned with *us* and *now*. It is committed to relevance and application for today, which is why I will offer a constructive approach to the topic in chapter 4.

One of the problems with contextualized preaching today, however, is that it often has a misplaced emphasis. By elevating contextualization to a studied discipline overly focused on practical gains, some preachers treat the biblical text in a haphazard and halfhearted way. This is the *blind adherence* problem. Out of a healthy desire to move the mission of his church forward, the preacher focuses his preparation exclusively on creative and artistic ways he can make his sermon relevant.

Think about it. Some preachers spend more time reading and meditating on our contextual setting than we do on God's Word. We get caught up in sermonizing about our world or city in an effort to be relevant. As a result, we settle for giving shallow impressions of the text. We forget that the biblical text *is* the relevant word. It deserves our greatest powers of meditation and explanation.

To put it differently, the preacher is bound to miss the mark of biblical exposition when he allows the context he is trying to win for Christ control the Word he speaks of Christ. As I stated in the introduction, this is the undoing of many of our churches. Too many of us unconsciously believe that a well-studied understanding of our cultural context, rather than the Bible, is the key to preaching with power.

Blind adherence to contextualization alters our preaching in at least three ways, and none of them is for the better. First, it impairs our perspective in the study—in his preparation of his sermon, the preacher becomes preoccupied with the world rather than God's Word. This leads to *impressionistic preaching*. Second, it changes our use of the pulpit—the Word now supports our intoxicating plans and purposes, rather than those of God. This is *inebriated preaching*. Finally, it shifts our understanding of authority—the preacher's "fresh" and "spirit led" devotional reading becomes the determinative point of truth. I call this *"inspired" preaching*.

Let's look at each of these a little more closely. I think we will find that some of what we think is expositional preaching actually misses the mark.

IMPRESSIONISTIC PREACHING

In the 1850s, the dominant artistic style of the moment was *realism*. It was a movement that aimed to represent, as closely as possible, what the artist had seen. Two young students being trained in realism were Claude Monet and Pierre-August Renoir. They had become friends and began to paint together, along with several others. This younger generation tended to use brighter colors than their realist instructors, and they favored painting contemporary life over historical or mytho-logical scenes, consciously leaving behind the romanticism of previous generations, as well.

The tipping point for helping these young painters to begin to self-identify as a group came in the 1863 *Salon de Paris* (Exhibition of Paris) art show and competition. So many of their pieces were rejected by the judges that an alternative show was held later, the *Salon des Refusés* (Exhibition of the Refused).[3] During the next ten years, the young artists peti-tioned to have ongoing alternative shows for their new styles of painting, but they were systematically rejected.

In 1873, Monet, Renoir, and several others formed an anonymous cooperative of artists to show their work inde-pendently. The first public exhibition of this new group oc-curred in April 1874 in Paris. Styles had shifted even further. Renoir had begun to experiment by altering the reality of what he saw—a distinct departure from realism. Monet had begun painting with looser brush strokes. This gave a general form of what he saw rather than a precise rendition, which was still preferred by the older generation. For example, his *Impression, Sunrise* captures the Le Havre Harbor at sunrise. Recognizing that it was not a realistic view of the harbor, he added the word "impression" to the title when asked for the name of the work. This title was later used by a critic to ridicule the artists, calling them the "impressionists."

One of the boldest innovations of the group was its use of light. For example, Renoir's 1876 *Dance at Moulin de la Galette* depicts a garden party with dancing in the Montmartre district of Paris. In the painting, Renoir paints white on the ground or on top of a blue jacket to indicate that the sun was shining there. The altering of light begins to exaggerate details and distort what would have actually been seen by the artist.

The impressionist method takes what the eye sees and interprets it, exaggerates it, ignores parts of it, and ultimately distorts it.

Now, think about what you do when you sit down to prepare a sermon. You open your Bible. You don't have a lot of time. You probably have a meeting or two tonight. You might have a family or a staff to guide. You certainly have your hands full with pastoral work. Yet you need something to say on Sunday. So you begin by reading your text and jotting down things on your computer the way an artist might interact with a canvas—quick-hitting, colorful connections between the Word and the world as you know it.

You are looking for things that you know will make an immediate *impression* upon your listeners. You begin enjoying this momentary diversion. The work is not hard. Soon a main idea emerges. You contextualize well since, just like your congregation on Sunday, you are not that passionate about things historical. In fact, you got this job, in part, because they were impressed with how well you produced attention-grabbing messages from the otherwise inaccessible ancient realism of biblical scenes. A detailed study of the text can wait.

This week's message, like last week's, will concentrate on the relevant impressions you draw from the passage. Applications already seem to emerge like beams of light for you to spread across the congregation in bold color. You glance at your iPhone to catch the time. You have been at work for fifteen minutes.

This is impressionistic preaching.

It happens a lot. In fact, it may be the most significant problem facing preachers today. Impressionistic preaching is not restrained by the reality of the text. It ignores the historical, literary, and theological contours of the text. It brushes past—in a matter of minutes—many of the exegetical tools you spent time developing. Where the realist painter might look at his object ten times before painting a single stroke, the impressionist looks at his text once and puts ten strokes on the canvas of human experience. So, too, the impressionist preacher.

There is no doubt that impressionistic preaching is easier and quicker. It makes more sense, given your busy schedule. But you need to know that it means, at the end of the day, you are doing whatever you want with the text.

Let's look at an example. Imagine that you have to prepare a message for your "young parents" class. You decide to speak on 1 Samuel 2:12–21. Take the time to read it now:

Now the sons of Eli were worthless men. They did not know the LORD. The custom of the priests with the people was that when any man offered sacrifice, the priest's servant would come, while the meat was boiling, with a three-pronged fork in his hand, and he would thrust it into the pan or kettle or cauldron or pot. All that the fork brought up the priest would take for himself. This is what they did at Shiloh to all the Israelites who came there. Moreover, before the fat was burned, the priest's servant would come and say to the man who was sacrificing, "Give meat for the priest to roast, for he will not accept boiled meat from you but only raw." And if the man said to him, "Let them burn the fat first, and then take as much as you wish," he would say, "No, you must give it now, and if not, I will take it by force." Thus the sin of the young men was very great in the sight of the LORD, for the men treated the offering of the LORD with contempt.

Samuel was ministering before the LORD, a boy clothed with a linen ephod. And his mother used to make for him a little robe and take it to him each year when she went up with her husband to offer the yearly sacrifice. Then Eli would bless Elkanah and his wife, and say, "May the LORD give you children by this woman for the petition she asked of the LORD." So then they would return to their home.

Indeed the LORD visited Hannah, and she conceived and bore three sons and two daughters. And the boy Samuel grew in the presence of the LORD.

In your first reading of the text, three things stand out:

1. The text presents you with two sets of parents and children: Eli and his worthless sons, and Hannah and her little Samuel, who is serving God.

2. You are impressed with the contrast between them. Eli's story reads like a manual on bad parenting, while Hannah's patterns get better results.
3. You land on two takeaways for your message. First, bad parents allow their kids to eat too much, while good parents don't. How repulsive it was for Eli's sons to gorge on sacrificial offerings! Second, bad parents don't take advantage of church settings to encourage their children toward godliness, while good parents are always present and available. How wonderful for Hannah to have Samuel at church whenever the doors were open!

There. You've got your outline. Most importantly, you know that your talk will resonate with the young parents in your congregation. After all, the news outlets in your city are reporting on the problem of physical conditioning among local children and the impending legislation to address it. It won't take much for you to contextualize similar principles that apply to their spiritual well-being as well.

You deliver your talk. The next thing you know, new children's programs are launched out of this sermon. Weekend retreats devoted to good parenting are planned. It's great, because people are talking about Christian parenting.

This kind of impressionist preaching is growing churches. It's really no wonder we don't spend time working on sermons. We don't need to. We can do this quickly and it works. It's almost improvisational preaching.

Then again, we also miss out on the richness of God's Word. We miss out on the point of the text. If we read it a few more times, we might realize that the primary concern of 1 Samuel

2:12–21 is not parenting at all. It's the holiness of God. That's right, *the passage is about God* and how the bad leadership of God's people makes a mockery of God himself. The problem in the text is that God is not being properly worshiped. And if we keep digging in the book, we'll realize that there is a replacement motif here within God's family. The text brings up Samuel precisely at this point because he is the alternative to Eli's sons for leading the worship of God in accordance with the Word of God. God can't get his work done because his Word has been undone. Even so, when the situation looks hopeless, God will raise up another man and priest to lead.

Does this mean we cannot preach parenting from this text? Not necessarily. But it means we must not miss the primary point of the passage. The possible applications must never overshadow the primary point of the text. While we can say true things from the Bible about parenting from this text, we should do so in a way that respectfully submits to the emphasis of the text. This is the difference. This is the challenge. We read these stories and end up missing what the Spirit is emphasizing while reducing God's Word to nothing more than principles for godly living. In the example from 1 Samuel, we ended up completely omitting Christ as the replacement for a failed priesthood. We lost Jesus to impressionism. And in his place we have parents who are more committed to moralism than to the Christian message.

It is important to note that impressionistic preaching is not *the* problem. It is a natural outcome of *blind adherence to contextualization* and how such an adherence monopolizes our time. We need to remember the conviction that restrained Charles

Simeon in the study: to bring out of Scripture what is there. It is easy to let an impressionistic approach dominate your study and preparation for preaching. Especially if you are intrinsically cool (i.e., fashionable or hip), or are trying to be, this approach can become the cocaine you snort in private. And if you have had a little success with it, you can begin to believe that you are an expositor. But as we will see in the coming chapters, biblical exposition requires a different approach in the study.

INEBRIATED PREACHING

Let's move out of the study and think about the way we use the Bible in the pulpit. Scottish poet Andrew Lang once landed a humorous blow against the politicians of his day with a clever line indicting them for their manipulation of statistics.[4] With a slight alteration in language, the quip could equally be leveled against many Bible teachers today: "Some preachers use the Bible the way a drunk uses a lamp post . . . more for support than for illumination."

This is the inebriated preacher. I suppose I don't have to tell you that you don't want to become one. The fact is, though, many of us have been one and just didn't know it.

Let me explain. On those weeks when we have stood in the pulpit and leaned on the Bible to support what we wanted to say instead of saying only what God intended the Bible to say, we have been like a drunken man who leans on a lamppost—using it more for support than for illumination. A better posture for the preacher is to stand directly under the biblical text. For it is the Bible—and not we who preach—which is the Word of the Spirit (see Heb. 3:7; John 6:63).

With decades of pastoral ministry now behind me, I can think of myriad times I have been the inebriated preacher. I have gone to the Bible to prop up what I thought needed to be said. It became a useful tool for me. The Bible helped me accomplish what I had in mind. At times, I lost sight of the fact that *I* am supposed to be the tool—someone God uses for his divinely intended purpose. I am to proclaim the light he wants shed abroad from a particular text.

What happened to me in the past can happen to any of us. There are a variety of ways we use the Bible the way a drunk uses a lamppost. Perhaps you have incredibly strong doctrinal views and these become the point of every passage you preach, regardless of what the text is conveying. Perhaps you draw political conclusions or social conclusions or therapeutic conclusions regardless of the mind of the Spirit in the text. In essence, our propensity for inebriated preaching over expositional preaching stems from one thing: we superimpose our deeply held passions, plans, and perspectives on the biblical text. When we do so, the Bible becomes little more than a support for what we have to say.

Let me give you a personal example of how quickly this can happen. Several years ago, I was preaching my way through 2 Corinthians. When I arrived at chapters 8 and 9, I decided to jump over them—forging ahead from chapter 10 onward. My reason for doing so was simple. I wanted to keep 8 and 9 in the bag for a later time in the life of our church. Those chapters are about money, right? I thought to myself, "The elders are going to come to me at some point and tell me to do a sermon on stewardship." At that point, our church was doing well financially. It made sense to save that text for a time when we would need a financial boost to keep ourselves solvent. So I skipped chapters 8 and 9—something that is rare for me as a rigidly sequential preacher.

Sure enough, the time came. I went to 2 Corinthians 8 and 9 to prepare a sermon on the importance of generous giving. Now, it is important for you to know that even before I entered into my study, I had a very clear idea of what I would say from the pulpit. I was going to center all my comments on the three verses that highlighted the cheerful giver:

> The point is this: whoever sows sparingly will also reap sparingly, and whoever sows bountifully will also reap bountifully. Each one must give as he has decided in his heart, not reluctantly or under compulsion, for God loves a cheerful giver. And God is able to make all grace abound to you, so that having all sufficiency in all things at all times, you may abound in every good work.

As it is written,

> "He has distributed freely, he has given to the poor;
> his righteousness endures forever." (2 Cor. 9:6–9)

First, I would open with the attitude that God wants us to have toward money. Verse 6 says that giving generously means reaping generously. (I loved starting with attitude because it connected my introduction to the application of "give!") After all, verse 7 says that God loves a cheerful giver. The motivation for giving (God will give back to you) would be my second point. Verse 8 says, "God is able to make all grace abound to you." Finally, I would address the quotation from Psalms to show the divine incentive for generosity. For, verse 9 appears to indicate that God himself "distributed freely." My three-point outline looked like this:

1. 2 Corinthians 9:6–7—Give to God (this is the attitude he wants from us).
2. 2 Corinthians 9:8—Get good things from God (this appeals to our motivation).
3. 2 Corinthians 9:9—Giving is a way we imitate God (the OT tells us so).

While I hadn't listened very long to the text, I knew that I had a sermon that would be easy to hear. I was well on my way to delivering a very practical and poignant message. I knew what our people needed, and the Bible proved my point.

But then something interesting happened. Before Sunday arrived, and before entering the pulpit to preach, I began to study the background to these chapters. And what I discovered shook the foundation of everything I had planned to say. From 1 Corinthians 16:1–4 and Acts 11:27–30, I learned that my verses had something to do with a famine and a need among certain churches. My cheerful-giving text was not about giving regularly to the budget of the local church. It was about a collection for famine relief for churches filled with Jewish Christians in a different part of the world.

If that weren't bad enough, I found other things, too. From 2 Corinthians 11:5 and 12:11, I learned that the primary dispute in the letter was over Paul's seemingly weak ministry in comparison to the super-apostles, who possessed the kind of power the Corinthian congregation respected. Paul was unskilled in speaking (11:6), came in humility (11:7), was always in need (11:9), and had no financial resources (12:14–15). This was the context of the chapters devoted to an offering. Then it dawned on me. This offering functioned as a test! If the Corinthians gave generously, it would demonstrate that they identified with "weakness" and were willing to meet the needs of those who were weak. If, however, they gave sparingly to the famine relief fund, it would prove that they aligned themselves only with those who have it all. I suddenly realized that I was in real danger of misunderstanding the whole book!

Then the whole thing caved in. When I looked at the psalm quoted in 2 Corinthians 9:9—the psalm that I thought taught us that giving generously means we're imitating God—I found that instead, it demonstrates that we are like "the righteous man." Paul's point was not that the Corinthians should give generously in order to imitate God. Rather, giving generously is the ordinary mark of those who follow God.

At this point I knew I was in trouble. While I had engineered a great outline from the Bible that accomplished my goal of addressing our budget shortfall, I was only leaning on the Bible the way a drunk uses a lamppost—more for support than illumination.

The only remaining questions I had to answer before stepping into the pulpit that week were: Who will be king? Me? Or the biblical text? Would I reign over it this week, or would it rule me? Would I lean on the Bible for my purposes and plans, or would I stand under it, allowing the illumination of the Holy Spirit to have his way with my people?

In the final analysis, the conviction that allowed Charles Simeon to exercise a mature restraint in the pulpit won the day for me. "I have a great jealousy on this head; never to speak more or less than I believe to be the mind of the Spirit in the passage I am expounding."[5]

From personal experience, I can say that my own struggles with inebriated preaching are always connected to a *blind adherence to contextualization*. And what I have learned is this: my congregation's needs, as perceived by my contextualized understanding, should never become the driving power behind what I say in the pulpit. We are not free to do what we want with the Bible. It is sovereign. It must win. Always.

Our role as preachers and Bible teachers is to stand under the illuminating light of the words long ago set down by the Holy Spirit. Our job is to say today what God once said and nothing more. For in doing so, he still speaks.

"INSPIRED" PREACHING

We have looked at two negative consequences that blind adherence to contextualization has for biblical exposition. First, we explored the impact this approach has on the preacher in his study. This method of preparation can lead to *impressionistic preaching*. Second, we looked at how blind contextualization can influence the preacher's use of the Bible in the pulpit. The weekly pressures for relevance can result in *inebriated preaching*.

Now I want to take the preacher out of his study and out of his pulpit and look instead at how he reads his Bible in private. For even here, the contemporary reading strategies that people adopt for their "quiet times" can impair the public proclamation of God's Word. In fact, if you combine these private reading strategies with a blind adherence to contextualization, you get something I call *"inspired" preaching*.

Let me explain. By way of divine authorship, the Bible is and always will be God's authoritative and inspired Word. Sadly however—and this is the point I am getting at—preachers are increasingly appealing to their subjective reading of the text as inspired. More and more, Bible teachers are being told that whatever moves their spirit in private readings of the Bible must be what *God's Spirit* wants preached in public.

One example of this kind of reading strategy has a long history. It goes by the name of *Lectio Divina*. This traditional Benedictine practice of scriptural interpretation was intended to promote communion with God and, to a lesser extent, familiarity with the Bible. It favors a view of biblical texts as "the Living Word" rather than as written words to be studied. Traditional forms of this practice include four steps for private Bible reading: reading, meditating, praying, and contemplating. You begin by quieting your heart with a simple reading of the text. Then you meditate, perhaps on a single word or phrase from the text, and in so doing intentionally avoid what might be considered an "analytical" approach. In essence, the goal here is to wait for the Spirit's illumination so that you will arrive at meaning. You wait for Jesus to come calling. Once the word is given, you go on to pray. After all, prayer is dialogue with God. God speaks through his Word and the person speaks through prayer. Eventually, this prayer becomes contemplative prayer, and it gives to us the ability to comprehend deeper theological truths.

It sounds wonderfully pious. In fact, it seems to have a solid scriptural warrant: "These things God has revealed to us through the Spirit. For the Spirit searches everything, even the depths of God" (1 Cor. 2:10). Setting aside for a moment what Paul was actually saying in this passage, *Lectio Divina* advocates a method that is spiritual as opposed to systematically studious. It substitues intuition for investigation. It prefers mood and emotion to methodical and reasoned inquiry. It equates your spirit to the Holy Spirit.

And *blind adherence to contextualization* loves it! What people today want more than anything is a "fresh word" from God, something from his Spirit that will nourish our impoverished spiritual lives.

While *Lectio Divina* is a historically Roman Catholic form of interpretation, it has found something of a resurgence in recent years, particularly among evangelical Protestants. And even where it is not practiced by name, it is remarkably similar to the way a lot of young preachers are taught to prepare. They are told to read the Bible devotionally, quietly, waiting upon the Holy Spirit to speak. For you can be assured that what God lays upon our hearts from a text in the quiet of the moment, he will use also in the lives of others. So, "Preach it! It must be inspired."

Let's take as an example one of those wonderful kitchen-calendar verses, Philippians 4:13: "I can do all things through him who strengthens me."

How do we approach this text? We start with reading it personally, as though Paul wrote it directly to us. Then we read "all things" as "anything." We think that of course this text is referring to anything. When we are faced with any kind of obstacle, God gives us the strength to overcome. Do I need this promotion at work? God gives me the strength. Do we need a three-point shot in these last twenty seconds to win the game? God gives the strength. What an inspiration! It's perfect for any of those moments when we need to succeed. And because we've understood the text devotionally, it's tempting to get into the pulpit and preach it that way.

The problem is, digging just a little deeper reveals that Paul is not talking about "anything." If we read just the few verses on either side, we realize that this verse is part of Paul's discussion about suffering in jail. He's talking about survival. He's not talking about promotions and game-winning shots, but about enduring hardship so that the gospel may advance (cf. Phil. 1:12). It doesn't take much to undo our very nearly inspired, very devotional reading. It just takes two or three verses.

This kind of "inspired" preaching is a dangerous game to play. It is completely subjective. When we stop the hard work of understanding the words that the Spirit has given us and work exclusively in the "mind of the Spirit," we become the final authority on meaning. We begin to lay down "truths" and "advice" that are biblically untestable or unsupportable. We may do so for good reasons, such as our sense of the moral health of our people or a genuine desire to renew the world we live in. But, nevertheless, we begin operating outside of orthodox doctrine. We confuse "thus sayeth the Lord" with "thus sayeth me." We ask our congregations to trust us instead of trusting the Word.

Now, you and I probably do not hold to this theory when it comes to the Bible. Yet subconsciously, we often work as if we do.

What does this look like? A lot of preachers—particularly young preachers—go to the text first for their own edification or spiritual growth. This is not an inherently bad practice, and devotional preaching is not inherently a bad thing. We all should be spiritually convicted by and conformed to the image of Christ in the text. The problem is that we are easily tempted to jump from the way the Spirit impresses the text upon us to how the Spirit must be working among our people. In this way, it's quite like impressionistic preaching, but dressed up in piety rather than practicality.

Just to avoid confusion, I am *not* saying that the Spirit has no role in expositional preaching. That would be a terrible mistake. While it is true that people are converted and matured through expositional preaching, the word of the gospel must be wedded to the Spirit's work in order for conviction of sin, regeneration, repentance and faith, and lifelong perseverance to come. Or to put it differently, "Neither he who plants nor he who waters is anything, but only God who gives the growth" (1 Cor. 3:7).

As it turns out, this "recent" collaboration between a devotional reading of the Bible and preaching—and especially its appeal to contextualization's desire to be spiritual—isn't as new as we might think. A version of it played out among theological figures like Karl Barth and the neoorthodox movement in the early part of the twentieth century. German higher criticism had "proven" that the text of the Bible had been corrupted, or so it was thought. And because the text had been corrupted, readers of the Bible couldn't authentically work their way back to the author's intent. Barth and the neoorthodox movement had a generally high view of Scripture, but conceded on certain points to the higher critics concerning verbal inspiration. Thus, in a neoorthodox church, the notion of responding to the Bible by saying, "This is the Word of the Lord," was no longer tenable. Rather, the reader might say something more like "Listen for the Word of the Lord." The assumption was that all we have left is the Spirit, therefore we'd better be listening to someone who has heard from him.

It's only a generation later, and some within evangelicalism are already moving beyond Barth for inspired or spirit-driven preaching. But are we trustworthy? The Holy Spirit is undoubtedly trustworthy and can, miraculously, implant his intent in us intuitively. But does this possibility absolve us from doing the hard work of exegesis? Why would he have bothered inspiring Scripture in the first place? Is it not possible that the Spirit works through both research and meditation? By pursuing such a subjective approach to interpretation as "inspired" preaching, are we not at risk of ignoring what God intended in his Word in favor of preaching our own? Are we not conforming ourselves to the spirit of the age (of which we are necessarily a part) rather than to the depth of his Word?

PUTTING THINGS TOGETHER BEFORE MOVING ON

Blind adherence to contextualization is a very real issue for preachers. It tempts us to uncritically and unrestrainedly pursue relevance, and these pursuits result in the shallowest possible work on the text. In this chapter we have looked at this problem from three angles. First, we explored what occurs in the preacher's study when the cultural context drives the sermon, rather than informs it. We end up displacing the realism of the biblical text for something *impressionistic* at best. Second, a blind adherence to contextualization often causes us to miss the mark of a proper use of the Bible in the pulpit. Many of us suffer from an addiction to practicality and the notion that we can predetermine what our people need to hear. When we do so, we imbibe from the tap of *inebriated preaching*. Third, a blind adherence is increasingly connected to a preacher's private devotional practice. Preachers want something "fresh" and "spiritual." And then we pass off our own spiritual or fresh feelings as the message of God. As a result, *"inspired" preaching* displaces expositional preaching.

We are right to ask: is there a simple way to express where our propensity toward contextualization ends up going wrong? I think there is.

The right side of this illustration shows the preacher's responsibility with the content of God's Word: *getting it right*. This is an essential part of our work. We all want to be faithful. The Bible gives us the words of the living God. The left side points us in another responsible direction: *getting it across*. This too is essential. Who among us doesn't want to be fruitful? The preacher stands in between these two tasks each week. They pressure him, each one wrestling for his time and attention. And more often than not, the preacher fears that a full commitment to one cannot be made without leaving the other behind.

As a result, the preacher begins to carry on conversations with himself that sound like this: "If I move in the direction of spending my preparation time *getting it right*, I'm afraid that I might end up being too heady, too intellectual, and lose the life impact of *getting it across*. After all, I can't afford to be known as a Word pastor if it means that I lose my identity as a Spirit-filled preacher. Don't I have a responsibility to speak to the heart, not just the mind? My messages need to show street credibility. I'm done with preachers who think only about spiritual conversion. I mean, orthodoxy is important, but without contextualization leading me in my work, I'll never get to orthopraxis. I know I speak from a text, but finally I'm here to make an impact today."

Whenever this argument emerges in the heart and mind of those called to preach—this sense that getting it right and getting it across are impossible partners—you can be assured that a blind adherence to contextualization is lurking nearby with impressionistic, inebriated, and "inspired" preaching ready to take the lead.

Of course, the two commitments to getting it right and getting it across are not impossible partners. Charles Simeon and every solid expository preacher I know have found a way to hold on to both. It is my hope that the next three chapters will show you an approach for preparing sermons that will enable you to join them in the faithful and fruitful work of biblical exposition.

2

EXEGESIS

We concluded chapter 1 by saying that it is possible to both "get the text right" *and* "get it across." We don't have to choose between one or the other. Both can be done, and done well.

But, how? How do we prepare messages that are both faithful to the text and fruitful for today? And how do we do it while avoiding our propensity toward a blind adherence to contextualization?

There is a way, and good expositors seem to take it. The next three chapters lay out a three-part process—a mind-set for working—that follows this course: (1) exegesis; (2) theological reflection; and (3) implications for today.

KEEPING FIRST THINGS FIRST

All preaching must begin with exegesis. To put it differently: contextualization, theological reflection, and matters of today are held at bay—we should be committed to a process of preparation that *keeps first things first*. By this I mean that a faithful preacher starts the sermon preparation process by paying attention to a biblical text's original audience and a text's purposes for those readers. And he makes this first audience his first concern in three different ways. In one fashion or another, he:

1. Gives the biblical context (rather than his own context) control over the meaning of the text.
2. Listens intently until he knows how the text fits within the overall message of the book.
3. Sees the structure and emphasis of the text.

Did you notice how nothing in the above list deals with contextualization? Contextualization is important, as we will see in chapter 4, but good biblical expositors train themselves to hold off on that step until later in the process.

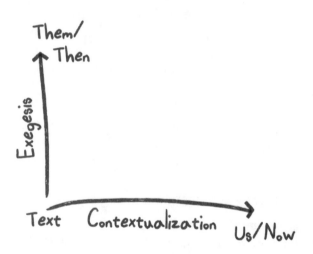

Contextualization is a good dance partner, but she should never be allowed to lead. Put her before the exegetical steps in your sequence of preparation, and problems will quickly emerge. The trouble is that too many of us push exegesis back in our preparation, and we clothe the message in a short red dress of contextualization by focusing on culture and our ability to connect with it. It's like we want to spin her out away from us in exciting circles, showing off her long legs and high heels.

For many of us, then, our greatest challenge will be to reorient what comes first. The first step toward expositional preaching is to treat contextualization like a woman you hold close. You lead her in the dance of exposition. It simply won't work the other way around. I can still remember where I was sitting on the day when this reorientation of mind-set clicked for me.

THE DAY THE PENNY DROPPED

I was twenty-nine years old when Steve Bickley, a pastor and friend, introduced me to Dick Lucas. Lucas is now retired as the rector of St. Helen's Bishopsgate Church in London. Bickley had arranged for Lucas to spend a day with those of us on the pastoral staff of College Church under Kent Hughes. This would be the day the penny dropped for me—and for all of us, really.

In short order, God used Lucas to challenge our conventional approach to sermon preparation. In two fast-moving hours, he put us in the world of a very familiar passage: 1 Corinthians 13. When he was done putting us through our paces, our preparation for preaching had found a new direction. He had set our feet on a better course, one that still guides me to this day.

First, Lucas asked us to *keep first things first*. This was harder to do than I had imagined. I had always heard 1 Corinthians 13 referred to as "the love chapter." My only exposure to it had been at weddings. On those occasions, the preacher's approach to the text—due to contextualization—was governed by the joyful event before us. Wedding days are ruled by the themes of encouragement and celebration, and the homilies I had heard on the text were likewise embedded with those sentiments. To put it another way, the audience in front of the preacher ruled the hour. Never mind the audience to whom the letter was first written.

Second, Lucas led us into a period of observation. He asked us to suspend judgment for a moment on what the text means or how it might be applied for today, but instead to consider the chapter in its *immediate literary context*. When we did, we saw that 1 Corinthians 13 was placed between two chapters that discussed spiritual gifts, and, in particular, the relationship between the gifts and spiritual maturity (12:1, 4, 9, 28, 30, 31; 14:1, 37).

Third, Lucas asked us to search out the terms for gifts and spiritual maturity earlier in the letter. He wanted us *to listen intently* until we knew how our text fit into the overall message of the book. That led us to 1:4–7, where Paul calls the Corinthians a gifted group. In fact, they did not lack any gifts at all. But in 3:1, Paul blasts this incredibly gifted congregation for being spiritually immature. He even calls them spiritual infants (vv. 1–2).

It was beginning to dawn on us that some in Corinth had gotten the relationship between gifts and maturity mixed up. They had begun to think that certain gifts ("tongues" in this case) gave them an advantage in spiritual maturity. Our minds began to race. What was Paul really saying about love in chapter 13? Did he mean to rebuke them for their lack of love? Was the Spirit's primary intention for the "love chapter" to correct rather than to encourage (in the guise of sentimentality)?

Fourth, Lucas showed us how the context of the whole book was wedded to the vocabulary of chapter 13. Think of chapter 13's "[love] is not arrogant." Does this language show up previously in the letter? It does, and Paul's prior use is not complimentary: "And you are arrogant!" (5:2).

Lucas then stopped and allowed us to take it all in. We realized that this chapter would have landed in the Corinthian congregation like a bombshell. Paul was talking about love precisely because it was the one thing the Corinthians lacked! They might have been a gifted group. But they were still infants. Paul wanted them to grow up, to be like him, a "man" marked by love, which for him was maturity.

We had arrived in Corinth—with the first audience—and ironically found ourselves better prepared to preach a relevant message for people in Chicago.

For me, the penny dropped right then and there. I could see the components necessary for any preacher doing exegesis. God powerfully used that day to reorder our approach to sermon preparation. All of us left that experience changed men. We had a renewed appetite for God's Word and a newfound commitment to what it would take to become expositors of the sacred text.

When the original or first audience becomes your first concern, you see things differently. Let me illustrate this with the telescope. Telescopes allow us to see far into the heavens. Galileo made them famous by using one to see craters on the moon as well as the millions or even billions of stars suspended in the Milky Way galaxy. The idea behind the invention is simple. Take two lenses, one larger than the other, and connect them with a sliding cylinder. The larger lens is curved with the capacity to magnify an image. The smaller lens is simply an eyepiece that allows the viewer to take a closer look at distant things. Hold a telescope the right way, and you will discover incredible things. But hold the telescope the wrong way, and the object in view suddenly appears distorted, small and out of focus. The beauty and shape of an object will be lost.

The same principle can be applied to your process of sermon preparation. If you want to be a good biblical expositor, you need to discipline yourself to put your eye on the original hearers first. This will keep you from distorting the shape of your text and help you to see what the Holy Spirit intends for your congregation.

That said, there's more to this than meets the eye. I don't believe I can do the exegetical work on my own. And so, each time before I sit down to study the Bible, I pray. For while there are ordinary means of study, I need the Spirit's extraordinary help in the process. And while I am going to share some practical things you can do in your study in the coming pages, you must understand that you are at the mercy of the Holy Spirit in understanding the text.

1. GIVE THE BIBLICAL CONTEXT CONTROL

In getting to the practical work, I have found it helpful to think about context in two different ways: *literary context* and *historical context*. These are two related and often overlapping ideas, but it is worth understanding the difference. The *historical context* concerns the circumstances or situation that prompted the text. This may require you to understand ancient culture. You may need to firm up your grasp of biblical history. Or you might study an entire book in an effort to piece together the situation faced by the first audience.

The *literary context*, on the other hand, is simply the text around your text. It considers an author's writing or editing strategy and asks why he has organized his book in the way he has. The verses or chapters that precede and follow a text give a flow or shape that helps us understand a text's meaning.[1]

Let's look at an example of how the meaning of a text should be controlled by its context rather than our own. In 2 Corinthians 6:14–15 we read:

> Do not be unequally yoked with unbelievers. For what partnership has righteousness with lawlessness? Or what fellowship has light with darkness? What accord has Christ with Belial? Or what portion does a believer share with an unbeliever?

There was a day when I might have preached a message from this text that was meant to help my people think through issues related to marriage or their choice of business partners. Indeed, this is the verse that spawns things like a Christian Yellow Pages.

The problem is, if we dig just a little deeper into the historical context, we will see that the writer is not talking directly to us. Paul had been arguing against the Corinthian affinity for securing popular and proud teachers who conducted their ministry in a way that avoided persecution at all costs. These "super-apostles" had led the people away from the gospel and away from Paul. And Paul wanted them back! He wanted them yoked to him. Historically speaking, therefore, our approach to this text should be controlled by Paul's concern about wedding ourselves to false teachers. It has nothing to do in the first instance with whom you marry or with whom you partner in business.

The literary context of these verses only confirms this. In the verses before, Paul tells the Corinthians that his heart has been open to them even while their hearts have been closed off. He pleads, "Widen your hearts" (6:13), an appeal to be closely yoked to him. And he returns to this plea in the verses following our passage: "Make room in your hearts for us" (7:2).

Knowing the historical and literary contexts can change everything for you. Good biblical expositors allow these contexts to control the meaning of the text. So, the first thing you should do is start reading the verses and chapters on both sides of your text. Start asking yourself a different set of questions. Why is this passage here in this place? How does my passage fit within a larger section? What is the situation faced by the first audience or, depending on genre, the first readers?

2. LISTEN FOR THE MELODIC LINE

At the outset of this chapter I mentioned that there are three practical ways of keeping first things first. Having looked at the first (giving the biblical context control), let's look at a second: listening intently to a text until we know how it fits within the overall message of the book.

The best preachers are usually the best listeners. They enter their studies with ears intent on listening. If that is our role, then we'd better learn to do exegesis with our ears as well as our mind! Every good expositor I know does exegesis by listening for the unique things that God is saying in the book they are expounding. Years ago, Dick Lucas represented the principle this way:

A melodic line is a short sequence of notes that form a distinctive portion of a song. It may be part of the main melody that gets repeated and varied. Books of the Bible work the same way. Each book has a melodic line, an essence that informs what the book is about. And each passage in the book, then, will serve that melodic line in some way. So, in preaching, we might ask, what is the essence of my book? And how is my particular passage informing it and informed by it?

The upside for preachers is this: if we know what the whole book is about, we can handle each individual passage better. There is also an important second benefit. If we make use of the melodic line in our preaching, our people will gradually learn what a book is about, even if they don't remember individual sermons.

How then do we find the melodic line of a book?

Let me tell you how I did it in high school. At several points, I was required to read a large book or novel. Inevitably, my teachers informed me that an exam was coming. And since the school library didn't stock CliffsNotes, I figured out how to get the main point of the book quickly. First, I looked for a paragraph somewhere in the introduction that offered some kind of thesis or purpose statement. Then I read the first and last chapters. Finally, I flipped back to the table of contents and, based on what I had read, tried to connect the dots between chapter titles.

I intuitively used different strategies to find the essence of the book: reading the book from *cover to cover*, reading and rereading the *beginning and end*, looking for important *repeated words, concepts, and phrases*, and hunting down *purpose statements*.

These same tools can help you find the melodic line of a book of the Bible. I discovered the benefit of adding this element to my sermon preparation a few years ago. I wanted to preach through the short book of Jude. I ended up preaching eight messages from it, and loved every minute of it. But getting the melodic line required some real effort.

Cover to Cover

Long before I began the Jude series, I incorporated the letter
into my private reading plan simply by reading it from start to
finish—not hard for a book of just twenty-five verses! I would
suggest doing this for any book you are going to preach. In fact,
it is always good to read it through in one sitting. The book
will start to become familiar. Getting to know it on its own
terms, listening intently to it, will pay great dividends when
you come to preach it.

Reading the Beginning and the End

A composer will often begin and end a piece of music with a
melodic line, even if he develops it throughout the piece. The
same is true for books of the Bible. When I knew that I was
going to preach through Jude, I spent time reading and rereading only the beginning and the end of the book. A single sound
began to emerge: *being kept*. In verse 1 Jude says he writes to
those who are "kept for Jesus Christ." And in verse 24 he refers
"to him who is able to keep you from stumbling." At this point
in my preparation, I felt ready to make a provisional guess as
to what Jude was about—*our being kept by God for Christ.*

Repeated Words, Concepts, and Phrases

At this point in the exegetical phase, I was ready to test my
provisional statement by tuning my ear to the content of the
letter. Did the idea of *being kept by God for Christ* play a significant role in shaping the body of the letter? I found that it did.
The same word used for *kept* in verse 1 (of which *keep* in verse

49

24 is a synonym) is repeated four more times: twice in verse 6 (the first time it is translated as "stay" in the ESV), once in verse 13 (as "reserved" in the ESV), and again as an imperative in verse 21. As exciting as this discovery was, the use of this repeated word challenged my initial melodic line! Those who are kept for Jesus at the beginning and the end of Jude are told in the body of the letter to keep themselves in the love of God. And this is in contrast to the fallen angels and false teachers who did not keep themselves and so are being kept in judgment. If at this point someone asked me what Jude was about, I would have said, *those who are being kept by God for Jesus have a responsibility to keep themselves in the love of God.*

Purpose Statement

Finally, I reread the letter in hopes of hearing a purpose statement.[2] It wouldn't take long to find one. Jude 3 captured my attention: "Beloved, although I was very eager to write to you about our common salvation, I found it necessary to write appealing to you to *contend for the faith* that was once for all delivered to the saints." This statement allowed me to hear the tonal quality of Jude. Whatever the melodic line, it needed to contain a sense of urgency. Nothing less than the health and holiness of the church was at stake!

Jude is anything but a dry theological ode that explores the themes of *kept* and *keeping* in terms of the relationship between God's sovereignty and human responsibility. No. This brief and potent letter is an impassioned piece of sheet music. My melodic line would need sharpening for a third time: *given the peril of the hour, the health and holiness of the church demand that those who are being kept by God for Jesus contend for the faith by keeping themselves in the love of God.*

I now had a melodic line. I had also learned two important lessons during this part of my preparation. Not only will I preach each individual passage better if I know how it relates to the overall message of the book, but also each listening strategy employed in this part of the exegetical process plays an important part in my overall understanding. A single tool for discovering the melodic line of a book just won't suffice.

3. SEE THE STRUCTURE AND EMPHASIS

In addition to giving the biblical context control and listening for the melodic line, biblical expositors do one more thing during the exegetical phase of preparation. They work to apprehend the skeletal structure of the text from which they are preaching. They ask: How has the author organized this text? What does the organization reveal about the author's intended emphasis?

In *How to Read a Book*, Mortimer Adler observes:

> Every book has a skeleton between its covers. Your job as an analytical reader is to find it. A book comes to you with flesh on its bones and clothes over its flesh. It is all dressed up . . . you must read the book with x-ray eyes, for it is an essential part of our apprehension of any book to grasp its structure.[3]

If Adler is right, then you cannot apprehend the point of a text until you have apprehended its skeletal structure. Put differently, good biblical exposition demands that you need to see the bones and the marrow of the biblical text for yourself.

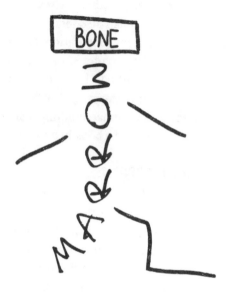

And when it comes to preaching, we can say even more:
Every text has a structure.
The structure reveals emphasis.
My sermon should be rightfully submitted to the shape and emphasis of the text.

This aspect of exegesis brings us back to the definition of expositional preaching that I gave in the introduction. It is empowered preaching that rightfully submits the shape and emphasis of the sermon to the shape and emphasis of a biblical text.

And for most of us, this is our problem. We step into the pulpit without apprehending the skeletal structure of the text. As a result, we are not very clear about the text's meaning, and when we step out of the pulpit, our people are no better off. How then do we find the structure of a text?

Use Reading Strategies That Work Well Anywhere

In trying to find the structure of a biblical text, you will want to start with simple strategies that are useful regardless of where you are in the Bible.

First, work from a word-for-word translation of the text. Of course, if you can study in the original languages, this will help you. But a word-for-word (rather than a thought-for-thought) translation generally renders individual words more consistently, which should make the bones more visible. That said, no single translation accomplishes this completely. You might find it helpful to consult multiple translations. Now, don't miss my point. We are talking about private preparation focused on finding structure. When it comes to preaching, there may be a variety of good reasons to use less literal translations.

Second, I have been helped by making my own translation of the text. The process slows me down, but I begin to see what the author is doing, and how each part relates to the larger unit.

Third, read, reread, and read the text again, slowly and out loud. The more time you spend in the text, the more you will see how it works.

Fourth, as you read, look for repeated words, phrases, and

ideas. If the goal is finding the structure and emphasis, frequently used expressions will usually be big clues in seeing the emphasis.

Know What Type of Literature You Are Studying

While some strategies work well throughout the Bible, the fact is, not all literature works the same way. You wouldn't pick up a newspaper and read it with the same tools you would use to read a poem. You wouldn't read a novel the way you would read a recipe. And you shouldn't read every book in the Bible the same way, either.

The Bible has different genres: Old Testament Narrative, Prophetic, Apocalyptic, Wisdom and Poetry, Epistles, Gospels, and Acts. Within those different genres, you have three basic text types: *discourse, narrative,* and *poetry.* As a general rule, you won't discover the structure of a psalm (poetry) using the same reading strategies you would employ in a Gospel (most likely narrative or discourse). Knowing how each of the different text types works will help you to know which tools best unlock them.

Generally speaking, *discourse* is spoken material. It is logical and linear. We find it most prominently in the Epistles. We also find it in the Old Testament history books, the speeches in Prophetic and Apocalyptic books, and the sermons in the Gospels and Acts. To find the structure in discourse, it is helpful to write the text out on a piece of paper without the paragraph breaks or verse numbers given by the editors of our Bibles. This is what I call getting the text out of the Bible. The important things to look for all relate to grammar. Look for repeated words or phrases, key words, transitional words, the flow of ideas, grammatical relationships, independent and dependent clauses, whether the text is written in the first (*I*) or second (*you*) or third person (*it*), whether it contains questions or declaratives or imperatives, and similar grammatical features. This is what we might call sentence diagraming. If you use these tools properly, you will normally find the shape and emphasis of your passage.

A *narrative* is a story, and stories tend to follow a fairly distinctive structure. So, while focusing on grammar can be helpful for an epistle, it is the *scenes, plot,* and *characters* that will assist the preacher in seeing the structure and emphasis of a narrative. Identifying different scenes—where the activity in the text changes location, for example—will probably be the best starting point. If you take longer narrative passages for your sermon text, the changes in scene will reveal an organizing principle. Within those scenes (and sometimes across scenes), you will want to look for plots. Plots typically have five parts:

- *Setting*: The setting will typically include place, time, season, and an introduction of characters.
- *Conflict*: Conflict is the part of the story that provides dramatic tension and a sense that something needs to be resolved. It might be very clear (like a violent threat), or it might be quite subtle (like emotional turmoil).
- *Climax*: The climax is the reversal or turning point, where the dramatic tension breaks.
- *Resolution*: The resolution is the outworking of the climax, how the conflict is resolved.

- *New Setting*: The new setting is the return to a new kind of normal from which the next plot arc will emerge.

In trying to identify these parts of the plot, the important questions to ask are: What is the conflict here? What is providing the dramatic tension? What is the turning point? How is the tension resolved? I would argue that the emphasis is located in some combination of the *climax* and parts of the *conflict* and *resolution*.

Of course, understanding how the author portrays the characters—the people in the story—is also important. Notice which people the author introduces and when. Notice how they change. Pay attention to how the author moves back and forth between them. If you have a good sense of the plot and the characters, you will have a good sense of the shape and emphasis of the narrative.

Poetry is a third text type. Most of the poetry in the Bible is in the Wisdom Literature and Prophetic Literature of the Old Testament. To find structure, you will want to consider repetitions of words or even entire stanzas (e.g., Psalms 42 and 43 are organized around the stanza that begins "Why are you cast down, O my soul?"). You will also want to consider changes in imagery and grammatical strategies (such as shifts in person or point of view). But probably the single most useful strategy for finding structure and emphasis in poetry is seeing how *parallelism* works in your text, particularly the transition between kinds of parallelism in the text. *Parallelism* is the technical term used for describing a feature of Hebrew poetry in which lines often appear in pairs (or sometimes triplets) that are related to or correspond to each other in specific ways. It may be that the second line repeats the general idea of the first, perhaps only slightly amplifying it. The second line may contradict, negate, or contrast the first. Or the second line might complete the thought of the first. These different relationships between the first and second line indicate different kinds of parallelism. Seeing the shifts in parallelism will help you find the shape and emphasis of your text.

THE DANGER OF THINKING YOU ARE DONE

Getting a good handle on both the general strategies and the genre-specific strategies will be a great start in finding the structure and emphasis of your text. And finding the context and the message of the book are equally important aspects of exegesis. Remember, you need to:

1. Give the biblical context, rather than your own, control over the meaning of the text.
2. Listen intently until you know how your text fits within the overall message of the book.
3. See the structure and emphasis of the text.

That said, I don't think you are yet ready to preach.

Exegesis is not enough. Done in isolation, exegesis alone can lead to preaching that is either overly *intellectual* or merely *imperatival*.

Intellectual preaching occurs when you make the first audience your final concern. It's what happens when you take a profoundly relevant text and render it irrelevant by writing sermons that read like an academic commentary. You do the work of exegesis but stop. You end up with boring, ineffective, well-footnoted speeches.

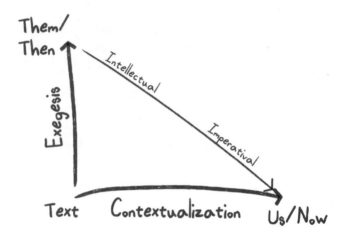

I encounter this kind of preaching particularly among young preachers who make the mistake of thinking that the sermon is—as my friend Mike Bullmore says—a storage container for housing everything they learned about the text that week. Well, it's not. You simply need to avoid preaching overly intellectual sermons.

The other pitfall of exegesis in isolation is that we become *imperative-only* preachers. The Bible is full of imperatives, and they are relevant. But imperatives without a proper biblical and theological context can also be applied in very wrong ways. Perhaps the most dangerous version of this is when we neglect the theological-reflection stage (which we'll look at in the next chapter). If we don't consider the gospel context of the Bible as a whole, even well-exegeted imperatives turn into moralism. And this fosters a legalistic culture in our churches.

All of this means that theological reflection is worth considering, which brings us to the next step in sermon preparation.

3

THEOLOGICAL REFLECTION

As we saw at the end of the last chapter, expositional preaching that stops with exegesis becomes merely intellectual or overly imperatival. It becomes academic or moralistic. The next phase of sermon preparation is still required: theological reflection. Without this, you are not yet ready to preach.

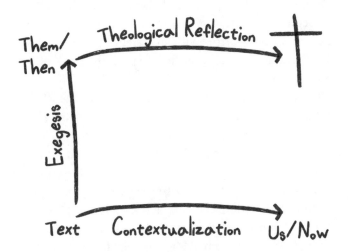

What is theological reflection? In simple terms, it is a rigorous and prayerful discipline of taking the time to meditate on my text and how it relates to God's plan of redemption. It is an exercise that asks how my passage relates to the Bible as a whole, especially to the saving acts of God in Jesus.

READING THE BIBLE WITH THE INSTINCTS OF JESUS

After his resurrection, Jesus anonymously joins some of his disciples on a seven-mile walk to a little town called Emmaus. As they walk, he demonstrates to these disciples how Moses and all the Prophets—all the Scriptures—concern him (Luke 24:25–27). Later that night he joins the rest of the Eleven and does it again; he opens their minds to understand the Scriptures and to see that what was written about him in the Law of Moses, the Prophets, and the Psalms must be fulfilled (vv. 44–45). He also tells these apostles that they will become witnesses and take this message and preach it to the whole world, starting with Jerusalem. The record of this proclamation is captured in the Gospels, the book of Acts, and the Epistles.

There is a principle here in what Jesus said. The whole of the Old Testament and the whole of the New Testament concern him and particular things about him. Verses 46–47 point to which particular things: "Thus it is written, that the Christ should suffer and on the third day rise from the dead, and that repentance and forgiveness of sins should be proclaimed in his name to all nations, beginning from Jerusalem" (cf. "suffering" and "glory" in Luke 24:26). To be sure, there is a lot of depth in that short sentence. The implicit kingdom rule in the word "Messiah" and the inclusion of "all nations" are incredibly rich ideas. Yet this simple sentence constitutes the heart of the gospel. The gospel, at least for Jesus, is found everywhere in the Bible. It is what holds the Bible together, and it should inform how we approach it.

READING WITH THE INSTINCTS OF PAUL

Importantly, this practice of proving Christ from all the Scriptures does not end with Jesus. It is modeled by Paul. In Acts, we read that "Paul went in, as was his custom, and on three Sabbath days he *reasoned* with them from the Scriptures, *explaining* and *proving* that it was necessary for the Christ to suffer and to rise from the dead, and saying, 'This Jesus, whom I proclaim to you, is the Christ'" (17:2–3). Acts records similar language of Paul in Athens (17:17), Corinth (18:4), and Ephesus (18:19; 19:8).

Paul's practice is conscious and rigorous. And as such, it is instructive for what is required of us in our reading of the Bible. First, the skills of reasoning, proving, and persuading marked Paul's approach when preaching Christ from all the Scriptures. Each of these terms has a rich background in Hellenistic moral philosophy and demonstrates a rigorous, thoughtful practice. Second, he employed these tools in diverse contexts—in the synagogue and the marketplace, in the presence of both Jews and Greeks. There were no shortcuts for one audience or another. Third, Paul found ways to preach this same gospel in settings where no biblical knowledge could be assumed. There is a way of preaching to people who lack a biblical background and vocabulary.

Paul, like Jesus, believed that the Scriptures pointed to Jesus's death and resurrection. Moreover, these three aspects of Paul's ministry indicate that theological reflection is a task that requires hard work.

READING WITH THE INSTINCTS OF SPURGEON

It might also be helpful to consider a more recent figure whose approach to reading the Bible puts Jesus in the center. The great Baptist preacher—the Prince of Preachers—Charles Haddon Spurgeon captured the idea this way:

> Don't you know young man that from every town, and every village, and every little hamlet in England, wherever it may be, there is a road to London? . . . And so from every text in Scripture, there is a road to . . . Christ. And my dear brother, your business is, when you get to a text, to say, "Now what is the road to Christ?" . . . I have never yet found a text that had not got a road to Christ in it, and if I ever do find one that has not a road to Christ in it, I will make one.[1]

Spurgeon has the right instincts. He's asking, how does my text anticipate or relate to the gospel? While I might not always agree with how he got to the gospel in his sermons from the biblical texts he was preaching, his question is the right one. And how we answer it is incredibly important.

Learning to reflect on your specific text in terms of Jesus and the gospel requires a working understanding of at least three distinct and influential disciplines. You can't make the journey toward becoming an expositor without them: the *historical-critical method*, *biblical theology*, and *systematic theology*.

THE CHALLENGE OF THE HISTORICAL-CRITICAL METHOD

If you are in an academic context like mine, a red light probably started flashing in your mind as soon as you read the word *theological* in the first paragraph of this chapter. And it should flash. After all, *theology* raises the problem of *history*. The difficulty with the historical challenge is that we often do not properly respect the exegetical side of our work. We give in to overly simplistic theological reflection, and either preach a shallow gospel tacked on to our text or preach doctrine instead of the text. This is a seriously bad place to be, at least if we preach this way weekly. It decouples Christianity from history.

If we preach in a way that treats the historical situation of our passage in the Old Testament as irrelevant and merely a springboard to the gospel, then we teach that the Bible is not really interested in history. History becomes a foil for theological dogma. At that point, we are only one generation away from an abstract and spiritual view of the resurrection rather than the historical view. We are one generation away from the Bible as moral mythology rather than Truth.

In other words, it is entirely possible for a new breed of evangelical preachers, out of a goal of preaching Christ from all the Scriptures, to undo the very foundation of Christian preaching.

This historical concern is not new. John Owen, when he first published his *Biblical Theology* in Latin in 1661, raised this issue. The first three chapters tackle the idea of "theology" as something that is superimposed on the text and history of the Bible. This concern remains with us today. Some notable academic divinity schools (including one in my neighborhood) still refuse to bring a *theologian* onto the faculty for this reason.

One of the clearest and ablest critics on the Christian desire to read everything through the lens of Jesus is James Barr, an Old Testament scholar who wrote mostly in the last half of the twentieth century. He looks on Christian (or Christ-centered) preaching with skepticism because it frequently does not allow the Old Testament to speak for itself. Rather, Christianity is imported to it, or imposed upon it—so much so that the Old Testament is silenced. According to Barr, "If Christianity is actually imported into it or imposed upon it, the effect will be actually to reduce the value of the OT for Christianity and its influence upon it. It should produce Christian results but should not be Christianized. But can this be done?"[2]

As skeptical as he is, Barr still frames the conflict as a question. Can it be done? Can passages from the Old Testament be preached as Christian texts without undermining what they meant in their original context? Barr's question is an important one.

I can only imagine what Barr might think of the simplistic way that some Christian preachers tackle the vision of God in Habakkuk 3. In that chapter, God appears in bright light, dressed as a victorious warrior. In descending to earth, God works a miraculous salvation for his people who have been tyrannized by their earthly enemies. For the beginning expositor—one who has *blind adherence to Christ-centered preaching*—this text is fulfilled in Jesus who works a mighty salvation for sinners. But Barr might ask: "What right do you, Christian expositor, have to declare that what God promised to Israel concerning her human enemies actually refers to victory for all people under the dominion of a spiritual adversary?" Has the young preacher just discarded history in favor of a *spiritualized* faith? Has he *dehistoricized* the text?

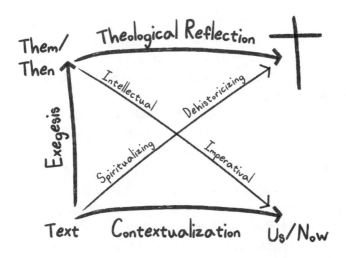

This example from Habakkuk 3 brings us back to the question of whether preachers can connect Old Testament passages to Christ without undermining what it meant for the original historical audience. Is there a way forward that follows the principle Jesus laid out in Luke 24—that all the Scriptures relate to his gospel—yet does not dehistoricize the text? Of course, we might also ask this question of the New Testament. It is so easy to get lost in the historical context of second temple Judaism or Greco-Roman backgrounds and never ask the question of how a passage really relates to the gospel. The challenge of the historical-critical method becomes one of *how*. How do we reflect theologically on a biblical text without compromising its historical integrity?

First and foremost, this question of theological reflection must begin with prayer. That is, the "work" of theological reflection can only be done through prayer. There is an intimate connection between the revelation of the identity of Christ—seeing him as the fulfillment of the Scriptures—and moments of prayerful quiet.

Luke makes this connection on a number of occasions. When Peter responds to Jesus's question, "But who do you say that I am?" with "the Christ of God," the readers had just been told that Jesus was praying alone (Luke 9:18–20). In other words, Luke wants his readers to know that Jesus was revealed to Peter in the context of prayer. The transfiguration, when Jesus was revealed in his glory as the Son, the Chosen One, follows Jesus taking Peter, James, and John to go to the mountain and pray (Luke 9:28–36). Back in the beginning of the Gospel, aged Simeon and Anna are both identified as pious people of prayer—statements that immediately precede God's revealing Jesus to them (Luke 2:27, 37; cf. Luke 2:28–32, 38). Even when God reveals the identity of Jesus at his baptism, Luke records that the heavens were opened and that God spoke, claiming Jesus as his Son. Luke records that the heavens opened just as Jesus was praying (Luke 3:21–22).

Luke could not have been any clearer: God reveals Jesus to people as a consequence of prayer. And so, if we really want Jesus to be revealed in our preaching—if we really want to uncover Jesus as the very center of all the Scriptures—then we must begin with prayer in our preparation. Only then can we begin a serious phase of theological reflection. Only then can we move into the work of biblical theology and systematic theology.

THE USEFULNESS OF BIBLICAL THEOLOGY

The discipline of biblical theology asks us to take a step back and look at the big picture of what God has said and done and see how it all relates to the epicenter of his revelation: the death and resurrection of his Son. I sometimes define the discipline as a way of reading the Bible that follows the progressive unfolding of God's redemption plan in Christ.

The discipline of biblical theology offers preachers a certain benefit. It prevents merely intellectual or moralistic preaching. To put that positively, it brings you—legitimately— to the heart of the Christian gospel from particular texts in the Bible. It keeps the main thing the main thing.

How, then, does biblical theology work? How do we use it legitimately in our expositional preaching? How do we make use of biblical theology in preparing sermons? I think there are three things we must do:

1. Get a biblical theology.
2. Follow the New Testament's lead.
3. Make good gospel connections.

1. Get a Biblical Theology

You can't use what you don't have, so the first step must be to get a biblical theology. And the best way to get one is to read the Bible consistently and completely. Nothing will prepare you to make connections better than having a deep and internal knowledge of the whole Bible. Make it a habit to read through the Scriptures regularly and prayerfully. Look for the melodic line as you read each book. The more you spend time looking at the big picture, the better your grasp of the big picture will be.

There are also good secondary sources for biblical theology. I cut my teeth with *Biblical Theology* by Geerhardus Vos. He understood the Bible to work in terms of epochs (Mosaic, Prophetic, and New Testament). I moved from Vos to Jonathan Edwards's *A History of the Work of Redemption*. He broke the story line into three historical periods as well: the fall to the incarnation, the incarnation to the resurrection, and the resurrection to the end of the world. Then I read Graeme Goldsworthy's *Gospel and Kingdom*. He understands "kingdom" to be the dominant theme holding the whole Bible together (I recommend that you start with Goldsworthy). If you want a simplified take, read Vaughan Roberts's *God's Big Picture*. If you want an even more simplified take—something at a six-year-old's level—read *The Big Picture Story Bible*.

Of course, as you develop your own biblical theology more broadly, you still need to make those connections in your sermon preparation on a weekly basis. But remember, we must do so in a way that respects the history and literature of the

Bible. It's not as simple as asking the question, where is Jesus in my text? He's not hiding under every rock or behind every tree. We need to start with slightly more nuanced questions. For example, you might start with:

- How does the gospel affect my understanding of the text?
- How does my text anticipate or reflect upon the gospel?

But better questions will not do all the work.

2. Follow the New Testament's Lead

The first biblical theologians—in the sense of uniting the testaments—were the New Testament writers. One can hardly flip a page in the New Testament without seeing an explicit reference to something in the Old Testament, not to mention the myriad allusions. Obviously, this is a huge help to anyone who wants to engage in biblical theology. The New Testament becomes something of a gold mine of biblical theological methods. If your text refers to or connects to another text (within the same testament or especially across testaments), then you have a good start. A great shortcut that I use almost every week is an index that comes with the *Nestle-Aland 28th Edition*. Even if you don't read Greek, this index is helpful because it lists every allusion and citation of the Old Testament in the New Testament.

I suggested earlier in this chapter that Paul's methodology in Acts points to the fact that it takes thoughtfulness and rigor to connect the Scriptures to the historical reality of Jesus's death and resurrection. But I think a quick look at his speech in Athens in Acts 17:22–31 offers a few ideas about how to make such connections. While the discourse does not expound a particular biblical text, it does reveal the gospel shape of the Bible. This shape is particularly evident in the way that Paul's sermon draws out certain theological categories.

Introduction

Paul turns iconic cultural objects into a conversation about God (vv. 22–23).

Body

Paul begins at the beginning, with God creating the heavens and the earth (v. 24a).

He reveals that humanity's universal problem is idolatry (vv. 24b–25).

He emphasizes God's eternality and desire to be in relationship with us (vv. 26–28).

He proclaims human culpability and calls for repentance (vv. 29–30).

Conclusion

Paul points to the resurrected Jesus as the One to whom our allegiance belongs (v. 31). He ends with God judging the world in righteousness (v. 31).

It takes Paul only eight verses to cover Genesis to Revelation. He moves effortlessly from beginning to end, from creation to consummation—speaking of God as Creator, humanity as fallen, Christ as resurrected, and Christ as returning in judgment on a day fixed in heaven. As such, this sermon provides a model for how we might effectively preach while moving through the grand sweep of biblical history in a short space. There is much to be learned from Paul's practice, wherever we are in the Scriptures.

These first two ways of using biblical theology in preparing our sermons lay an important foundation. You will need to have a biblical theology, an understanding of the whole Bible and how it fits together. And you will need to understand how the New Testament relates to the Old Testament and how the Old Testament anticipates the New. But—and this is important—you will need tools to make specific connections even when New Testament citations do not pave the way.

3. Make Good Gospel Connections

If what I have argued in the last few sections is right, then the challenge comes in making good gospel connections from the text you are preaching. Here are four categories of connections that I think will help you engage in biblical theological reflection:

> Prophetic fulfillment
> Historical trajectory
> Themes
> Analogies

Admittedly, these categories overlap significantly. The prophetic fulfillment may be through a theme or an analogy. An analogy may make use of a theme. A theme may include some sense of historical trajectory. There may be other distinct categories. The important thing is not taxonomy, but legitimacy. These categories are simply a starting point.

Look for Prophetic Fulfillment

Probably the clearest connections are the ones made explicitly. No doubt, you know that at certain moments in the Old Testament, God makes a promise about the Messiah who is to come. And in the New Testament, the writers pick up these prophetic moments and show how they were fulfilled in the identity and activity of Christ Jesus.

One of the easiest examples of prophetic fulfillment to see is Matthew's use of the word *fulfill*. At ten or eleven points in his Gospel, he breaks into the narrative to observe that Jesus fulfilled what one Old Testament prophet or another had spoken. From fleeing Egypt to Jesus's use of parables (Matt. 2:14–15; 13:35), much of Jesus's life directly fulfilled Old Testament prophecy. In fact, Jesus himself makes this point very near the climax of the Gospel:

> "Do you think that I cannot appeal to my Father, and he will at once send me more than twelve legions of angels? But how then should the Scriptures be *fulfilled*, that it must be so?" At that hour Jesus said to the crowds, "Have you come out as against a robber, with swords and clubs to capture me? Day after day I sat in the temple teaching, and you did not seize me. But all this has taken place that the Scriptures of the prophets might be *fulfilled*." Then all the disciples left him and fled. (Matt. 26:53–56)

Matthew's strategy of drawing the straight lines of prophetic fulfillment between the Old Testament and Jesus is simple enough. Luke's and John's Gospels also use this strategy. And it becomes a part of the apostolic method for ministry in the early church. For example, Peter's sermon in Acts 3 includes an important apologetic: "But what God foretold by the mouth of all the prophets, that his Christ would suffer, he thus fulfilled" (Acts 3:18; cf. 13:27). James also draws on this strategy when talking about Abraham's justification by faith (James 2:23).

Of course, this method of connecting works the other way as well. You may start with the Old Testament and see the explicit fulfillment of promises in Christ Jesus in the New Testament. For example, Moses tells Israel that God will raise up another prophet like himself who will bring God's Word; Peter then tells us that Jesus fulfills this promise (Deut. 18:15–22; Acts 3:22–26).

Look for Historical Trajectory

A second way to connect your text to the gospel is to look for historical progressions or *historical trajectories*. As with prophetic fulfillment, searching for a text's historical trajectory depends on the idea that God reveals himself progressively, and so redemptive history possesses a direction or trajectory that culminates in the cross. But this particular strategy requires us to look for the singular historical plot or story of redemptive history and to mark out pivotal points.[3] For example, we might summarize redemptive history as: Creation → Fall → Redemption → New Creation. A biblical passage might refer to one of these in such a way that we can place our passage within redemption history. Connecting a text to the gospel becomes as simple as showing where it falls on this story line.

This method is fairly simple. To draw an arc in computer programing, you need at least three points of reference. It's a matter of geometry. In the same way, to draw a historical trajectory in the Bible and see how it relates to the gospel, I think you need three points. I find it is easiest to take my passage and plot out a prior point in redemptive history as well as a later point in redemptive history that connects to my passage. This gives me three points in redemptive history. From here, I have a historical trajectory that shows me how my text relates to the gospel.

For example, Ecclesiastes 12:1–8 places a strong emphasis on remembering the Creator. So does Romans 1. Both of these passages point to a specific point in redemptive history from which the rest of redemption history flows. You can go back in Scripture to actual creation (Genesis 1–2) or forward to the idea of new creation (2 Cor. 5:17); both are periods of redemptive history that can connect you to the center of redemption. This way of connecting texts is especially useful when your passage has eschatological content or an apocalyptic tone. New creation itself includes the fullness of Christ's return and all its implications.

Look for Themes

Another way of connecting the whole of the Bible to the gospel is through biblical theological *themes*. God progressively reveals himself through certain themes, or motifs, throughout Scripture. While we generally recognize at least a couple dozen, some of the big ones include kingdom, covenant, temple/priest/sacrifice, and exodus/exile/rest.

Understanding how themes work is important. For example, while the exodus is a historical event recorded in the book of Exodus, it also introduces a repeated idea throughout Scripture: God delivers his people from slavery, through trials, to the place of his blessing. When the Prophets start to describe the exile and the return from exile, they describe it as a "new exodus." This theme of exodus, then, finds its ultimate fulfillment in Christ's death and resurrection (cf. Luke 9:30–31).

I remember one occasion when I was working in Luke 22:14–30. The theme of *kingdom* seemed obvious enough. After all, the word appears four times, and it's a dominant theme in the rest of Luke. But as I read, another theme caught my eye: covenant. Consider, "And likewise the cup after they had eaten, saying, 'This cup that is poured out for you is the new covenant in my blood'" (v. 20).

Covenant appears in Luke only twice, here and in 1:72. So I began working through the various covenants in Scripture. From Noah to Abraham to David, *covenant* is an important and abundant theme. This reference in Luke, of course, was more specific. This was not just any covenant, but a "new covenant." The new covenant is also connected to the Last Supper in 1 Corinthians 11:25, but it really brought me to Scripture's first use of the phrase, found in Jeremiah 31:31–34.

> Behold, the days are coming, declares the LORD, when I will make a new covenant with the house of Israel and the house of Judah, not like the covenant that I made with their fathers on the day when I took them by the hand to bring them out of the land of Egypt, my covenant that they broke, though I was their husband, declares the LORD. For this is the covenant that

I will make with the house of Israel after those days, declares the LORD: I will put my law within them, and I will write it on their hearts. And I will be their God, and they shall be my people. And no longer shall each one teach his neighbor and each his brother, saying, "Know the LORD," for they shall all know me, from the least of them to the greatest, declares the LORD. For I will forgive their iniquity, and I will remember their sin no more.

Understanding the new covenant connection to Jeremiah 31 was helpful because it led me to at least three other connections that aided my preaching. First, the emphasis that emerges in Luke concerns the ethics of the kingdom. In Jeremiah 31:34, God talks about the fullness of those benefitting from the new covenant as the "greatest" and the "least." In Luke, Jesus refers to this motif frequently (see 7:28 and 9:48; it also shows up as the *last* and the *first* or as a kingdom ethic of becoming humble in 13:30; 14:11; and 17:7–10). And in the very passage I was studying in Luke 22, Jesus tied the benefits of the new covenant to the ethic of discipleship as service—as becoming the least rather than the greatest (vv. 24–27).

The second connection that enhanced the sermon was one of participation. Not only was God making a covenant, but he was assigning a kingdom through covenant. The language of covenant, and particularly the verb "to make," in Jeremiah 31:31–34 is related to the verb *assign* in Luke 22:29. "You are those who have stayed with me in my trials, and I *assign* to you, as my Father *assigned* to me, a kingdom, that you may eat and drink at my table in my kingdom and sit on thrones judging the twelve tribes of Israel" (Luke 22:28–30).

Third, like the disciples, we do not need to be concerned with being the greatest (Luke 22:24). Jesus promises aspects of his rule to us in 22:30. Interestingly, the context of Jeremiah 31 focuses on a united Israel, in which the tribes are treated as a single entity that holds judgment over the whole world (see esp. Jer. 25:17–29).

As a result of making these connections between Luke 22 and Jeremiah 31 through the theme of covenant, my ability to preach Luke 22:14–30 was greatly enriched. The sermon wasn't merely about the Lord's Table, but it became about the ethics of our kitchen tables. It wasn't just about the covenant God made for our salvation, but it showed a covenant in which I participate and exercise rule.

Look for Analogies

One of the strategies most commonly used and misused by preachers is that of *analogy*. On the one hand, this branch of biblical theology might seem intimidating, because it requires distinguishing between analogy, typology, allegory, metaphor, and a variety of other technical terms. Of course, I would caution you against becoming too enamored of the technical terms, if only because different scholars and preachers define them in different ways.

What's more, it's easy to go overboard. Once you become comfortable with the jargon of, say, typology, everything you see gets framed in typological terms and everything you preach gets squeezed into an ill-fitting jumpsuit of typology, whether it actually is or is not typology.

Analogy is a broad category for comparing or contrasting

two things. Good stories are recognized as such, in part, for their ability to front-load characters or objects with traits or functions that take a great significance later in the story. It's what makes us want to reread a book or watch a movie for a second time. Early details, unknowingly glossed over on the first time through, become significant only after the author's hidden intention is finally made known. As the proverb says, "It is the glory of God to conceal things, but the glory of kings is to search things out" (Prov. 25:2). It would appear that God, in his infinite wisdom, endowed the very lives of certain individuals, objects, and events in Israel's history with analogical meaning which finds its fulfillment in Christ. Learning to recognize these correspondences in the Bible is essential to good exposition.

These correspondences may be broad—in which cases we simply call them analogies—or they may be narrow. When a person, event, institution, or object in the Bible narrowly anticipates some aspect of Jesus Christ, we call this *typology*. Typology is prophetic and escalates in significance.[4] For example, if King David is a type of Christ, then David (called the *type*) corresponds to Jesus Christ (called the *antitype*) through kingship, in which the meaning of kingship escalates in significance. Jesus is like David, but Jesus is greater than David.

Let's look at an example. In my church in Chicago's Hyde Park neighborhood, which is right next to the University of Chicago, we preach along the academic year. Because we have so many people who leave for the summer, it makes sense that we set apart summertime for special sermon series. A few summers, we decided to preach through 1 and 2 Samuel.

And I had the privilege of preaching from what I have come to believe is one of the darkest chapters in the Bible: 1 Samuel 28.

It was at the end of the chapter that the idea of analogy really came alive for me.

> Then Saul fell at once full length on the ground, filled with fear because of the words of Samuel. And there was no strength in him, for he had eaten nothing all day and all night. And the woman came to Saul, and when she saw that he was terrified, she said to him, "Behold, your servant has obeyed you. I have taken my life in my hand and have listened to what you have said to me. Now therefore, you also obey your servant. Let me set a morsel of bread before you; and eat, that you may have strength when you go on your way." He refused and said, "I will not eat." But his servants, together with the woman, urged him, and he listened to their words. So he arose from the earth and sat on the bed. Now the woman had a fattened calf in the house, and she quickly killed it, and she took flour and kneaded it and baked unleavened bread of it, and she put it before Saul and his servants, and they ate. Then they rose and went away that night.
> (1 Sam. 28:20–25)

Saul was at the end of his life. He had just had the medium of En-dor conjure up the ghost of Samuel so that Samuel could pronounce God's judgment on Saul, as he had done in chapter 15. Samuel told Saul that the next day his life would be over. And so Saul, along with his servants and the medium, broke bread. He was reluctant at first, but ultimately Saul, desperate for a word from God, obeyed the word of the medium. They celebrated with unleavened bread and a fattened calf. The next day, Saul fell on his sword and died.

The analogy is so intriguing. We have, on the one hand, the opposite of a Passover meal. Saul and his sons are staring at an irreversible death sentence of judgment. At the same time, we have a remarkable contrast to the Last Supper. Saul sat down to a meal with his small band of followers on the night before he would be killed, as Jesus would later do with his disciples. Together, they broke bread. And the point of the analogy becomes clear. Saul is a type of Christ—or really a type of anti-Christ. This night in his life anticipates, by way of contrast, the night in which Jesus broke bread with his disciples, the night right before he was killed as "a ransom for many." Some might point to a typological connection between Saul and Christ. Others might argue that there is a theme or typology of Passover here. However you categorize the correspondences, the analogy between the two situations greatly deepens our understanding of 1 Samuel 28 and how it ultimately is reversed in the glorious sacrifice of Jesus Christ.

With these tools in hand, hopefully you see how powerful biblical theology is for preaching Christ from all the Scriptures. Remember, there are three important things you must do in order to make use of biblical theology. First, get a biblical theology to use as a foundation. Second, whenever you can, follow the New Testament's lead in interpreting Old Testament passages. And third, start using these four tools to make good gospel connections.

THE ROLE OF SYSTEMATIC THEOLOGY

Biblical theology is a great starting point for theological reflection. And if you develop your biblical theological skills for preaching through plenty of experience, it will take you most of the way through this stage of preparation. At the same time, another branch of theology has a role to play in theological reflection: systematic theology.

If biblical theology helps you to discern the progressive unfolding of God's redemption plan in Christ, then systematic theology helps you to synthesize everything that the Bible says in the form of doctrines. It organizes Scripture logically and hierarchically, not historically or chronologically (as you would in biblical theology). D. A. Carson defines systematic theology as "the branch of theology that seeks to elaborate the whole and the parts of Scripture, demonstrating their logical (rather than merely historical) connections."[5]

At the same time, I think caution is in order. For while I advocate for the role of systematics in preaching, there is a difference between this and teaching systems. Simeon put it this way: "God has not revealed his truth in a system; the Bible has no system as such." The result of this conviction, then, is simple: "Lay aside system and fly to the Bible; receive its words with simple submission, and without an eye to any system. Be Bible Christians, not system Christians."[6] Simeon is right. We should not be system preachers. Still, there are three practical benefits of incorporating systematic theology into your theological reflection.

1. It holds you in the faith.
2. It helps you connect to the gospel from particular genres.
3. It hones your ability to speak to non-Christians.

1. It Holds You in the Faith

A major benefit of reflecting on systematic theology in your sermon preparation is that it provides a constraint. It holds you to orthodoxy. When you do your exegesis, you will inevitably come to difficult passages, forcing you to make difficult exegetical choices. And because none of us is perfect, we will make mistakes. When you begin to wrestle with these difficult conclusions about your text, sound doctrine will be a guide.

For example, a superficial exegesis of James 2:14–26 might lead you to conclude that James undermines Paul's doctrine of "salvation by faith alone." By submitting your work on that passage to systematic theological reflection, you will have to wrestle with how Paul's articulation of salvation works *with* and not *against* what James is saying. And even if you do not solve all your problems, you will at least be grappling with how Scripture helps to interpret Scripture rather than unknowingly pitting Scripture against Scripture, and, in so doing, denying an orthodox understanding of the inerrancy of Scripture.

2. It Helps You Connect to the Gospel from Particular Genres

The fact is, sometimes it is more challenging to make use of biblical theology in certain genres. The nature of biblical theology—a grand story—connects well to genres where narrative is the primary form of the text. At the same time, Old Testament poetry may not give you a legitimate window into the big story of the Bible the way you might hope. New Testament Epistles, which contain logical arguments, might also be difficult to connect through biblical theology.

Genres that have a lot of discourse or poetry might, however, be more easily connected to the gospel through systematic theology. These genres tend to more frequently address fundamental concepts like faith, grace, justification, sin, and the like. So when a psalm makes a point about repentance from sin, or Paul talks about faith and works, we have a legitimate window into the theological concept of the gospel.

3. It Hones Your Ability to Speak to Non-Christians

I would guess that most of the non-Christians walking into our churches are not like the Ethiopian eunuch—strongly and sincerely desiring to better understand Isaiah. Rather, I bet they are more likely to ask questions about the problem of evil, God, guilt, redemption, and the like. The answers to these questions flow from systematic categories. And so, legitimately connecting your text to systematic theology in the course of your sermon may actually be the best way to draw a non-Christian into the Word of God. For example, suppose a non-Christian is listening to your sermon and has questions about the notion of "sin" in your text. A helpful way of instructing on sin might be to look at this systematic category and realize that there are three major metaphors for sin: weight, debt, and stain. So, while your listener may not initially understand the idea of "sin" as it is there in your particular passage, you might incorporate the broader doctrine of sin into your sermon in a way that helps him.

ONE MORE STEP

In this chapter, we have covered a lot of ground. Hopefully, you see the value of not going directly from exegesis to application, or even stopping with just exegesis. Rather, I hope you see the value of spending time reflecting on how the point of your text might draw you to the gospel. A right understanding of the historical-critical method and the tools of biblical theology and systematic theology will move you forward in your work.

But, of course, we're not done yet. The challenges and demands of *today* still await us.

4

TODAY

The final phase of sermon preparation takes us to *today*. We arrive, at last, in the present. Behind us lie the hills of the ancient text and the exegetical work we did on "them and then." The distant line of theological reflection is also there, complete with its emphasis on the fullness of time in Christ Jesus, his death, and his resurrection. And straight before us is the destination: *today*. Us and now. The church. God's people, and those who, through the preaching of the Word, are to become his own.

Up to this point in the journey we have intentionally held contextualization at bay. We have done so because of its tendency to dominate our work—what we called *a blind adherence* problem. But with the biblical and exegetical work complete, we are ready to allow contextualization its rightful and necessary place at the table. While a healthy gospel ministry is always textually driven, it must be contextually informed. Contextualization should inform how we preach God's Word today along three lines:

> The Makeup of Your Audience
> The Arrangement of Your Material
> The Application of Your Message

It might be helpful to think of this final phase as a *synthesis*. The word *synthesis* comes from the ancient Greek and carries with it the idea of placing two or more distinct elements together in ways that form a new and coherent whole.

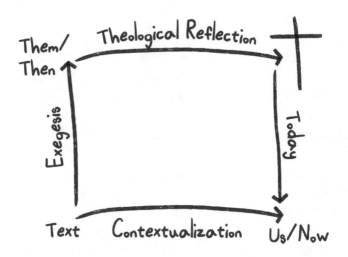

Many young preachers find this final leg of the journey difficult. They are not sure how to navigate it, or at least how to navigate it well. They might tackle the various parts in isolation. Some will certainly be able to complete the tasks of the exegetical process. Others might have adopted reading strategies that lead them into theological reflection. But if you ask how they go about placing two or more of those elements together in a way that forms a coherent message for *today*, things get quiet.

Yet synthesis must be done. And the biblical expositors who do it well, do so, in part, because of the contextualized attention they give to *audience*, *arrangement*, and *application*.

1. THE MAKEUP OF YOUR AUDIENCE

In the broadest sense, our attempts at contextualization must always avoid one of two mistakes. On the one hand, if our preaching always opposes culture, our message will be rejected by the world even before we have the opportunity to present Christ. On the other hand, if we accommodate our message for the world (or assimilate the pattern of our lives), we forfeit the very ground that enables us to be useful to God in the world. Our task is to find a way to take God's unchanging message into a world nearly void of biblical categories and rife with theological confusion.

While it is good to advocate for exegetical and theological work, good expositors never lose sight of the fact that those disciplines exist to serve people. I bristle at the mind-set some preachers seem to have—that the congregation is there to serve them in the exercise of their Word ministry. Younger preachers especially ought to be aware of this temptation toward establishing a self-serving ministry.

Over the past fifteen years, our church has been privileged to train more than seventy interns—young men and women heading toward full-time Christian service of one kind or another. Occasionally I will remind them: *the people are the point!* And if those who specifically desire to preach the Word do not possess a heart for the people of the world, they should not be allowed to stand regularly behind the preaching lectern.

So, if you want to become a biblical expositor, know this: a prerequisite for preaching is a growing and godly passion for people. Learn to know and love the audience God has given you. Isn't this the very lesson Jesus instilled in Peter before turning him loose on the world with the gospel? In John 21, Jesus appeared for the third time to Peter and the other disciples on the shores of the Sea of Galilee. Three times Jesus asked him, "Peter, do you love me more than these?" And three times, with increasing frustration, the soon-to-be preacher said, "Yes, Lord, you know that I love you." In response, Jesus told him, "Feed my lambs. . . . Tend my sheep." The point being driven home was clear: those whom Jesus sets apart to proclaim the gospel are those who demonstrate their love for him by loving his church!

And so I say to all of you who would desire to preach messages for Christ: Do you love Jesus? Do you really love him? Then manifest your love for him by feeding and tending those for whom he died. Learn to love people.

The Church

The primary audience for God's Word preached expositionally is the church, God's people. Faithful biblical expositors are always mindful of this. They labor over God's Word with great care, precisely because they know that the Word they proclaim saves and strengthens the church.

It was for his own people that God, in the garden of Eden, sent forth his Word. At Mount Sinai, God again called down his Word, this time inscribing it in stone so that his newly saved people might know him and his gracious ways. And when he sent forth Jesus, the very Word of God, he did so to gather a people to himself. At Pentecost it was the same. The communion of saints, those early ones who devoted themselves to the apostles' teaching, was converted through the preaching of the Word.

To put it as simply as I can, every faithful biblical expositor I know carries within himself the fixed conviction that the Word of God creates and sustains the people of God, his church.

How will this inform your preaching *today*? Expositors especially must be keenly aware of their need for an *audience* with God. He alone can accomplish the magnitude of the work set before us. We need to bring all our sermon preparation before God in prayer. It would be a mistake to think that preaching can be done in isolation—as if God's great and glorious work of converting and establishing his church rested upon our activity. We who preach must become those who pray. This alone is a sure indication that we understand how the church comes into being and blossoms in the world. And it causes us as expositors to prepare messages on our knees as well as from behind the study desk. By experience, we know what it is to plant our faces in the floor and plead for God to accomplish the work that our best efforts in preaching cannot.

In a word, we are desperate—desperate for the power of the Holy Spirit to attend our preaching. And so we pray. We pray in advance of preaching. We pray in the act of preaching. We pray even after our preaching is done.

The City

Much has been written in recent years about where our audience can be found. Not much more needs to be said here.

Suffice it to say, we are fast approaching a moment in human history when half the world's population will live in cities. Biblical expositors should not be ignorant of this fact. Rather, our preaching should be informed by it.

One need not succumb to the idiotic notion that God loves people who live in cities more than he loves people who don't. We simply need to attend to the challenges and opportunities of life in the city. The congregations to which many of us are preaching will be, by nature, more diverse in background and replete with competing worldviews that—if we are not careful with our words—could be an unnecessary cause of combustion. Our preaching should have a more diverse audience in mind, which means we should be willing to trade in the colloquialisms and inside jokes of our own little subcultures. You wouldn't address the city council with the same stories you would tell a close friend over lunch. It's a matter of reorienting our scope. We should preach as though we intend to be understood by people from the four corners of the earth precisely because, in many cases, those will be the people within the sound of our voice.

As God continues to assemble increasingly diverse congregations, two strategies for preaching should prove helpful:

An Interpersonal Strategy
An Integrated Strategy

For both of these, Paul's Athenian discourse is instructive. First, on the *interpersonal* front, Luke states that Paul reasoned and conversed with Athenians, both in the synagogue and the marketplace. In other words, his proclamation was not one-dimensional. We should not think of him merely as standing behind a lectern once a week delivering a monologue. Rather, he employed a variety of interpersonal strategies. In the marketplace he would even engage in a dialogical style. We, too, should look for ways and places to replicate this interpersonal strategy in cities today.

Also relevant to our interpersonal strategy: it appears that Paul didn't put himself forward but waited until he was given opportunity to speak to powerful people, at least in Acts 17. Luke records that "they took hold of him and brought him to the Areopagus, saying, 'May we know what this new teaching is that you are presenting?'" (17:19). The phrase "they took hold of him" is informative. Paul, it seems, was not presumptuous. He didn't force his way into the center of Athenian society. He didn't demand an audience among the elites. Rather, he went to his normal perches for preaching: the synagogue and the marketplace (v. 17). His sermon at the Areopagus was requested. Certainly we are to be bold, but the city will also demand respect from us.

Second, the growing significance of cities requires an *integrated strategy*. An integrated strategy, as opposed to an iconoclastic one, brings together cultural norms and the Christian message, utilizing them in ways that serve your proclamation of the gospel. An illustration of this occurs in Acts 17 where Luke, among other things, effectively clears Paul of any false charge of fundamentalist zealotry. He describes Paul as righteously provoked by the Athenian idols, but unwilling to overturn them in the streets. In fact, he shows Paul doing just the opposite—using them to his own apologetic advantage: "Men of Athens, I see that in every way you are very religious. For as I passed along and observed the objects of your worship, I found also an altar with this inscription, 'To the unknown god.' What therefore, you worship as unknown, this I proclaim to you" (vv. 22–23). By opening his message with "the unknown god," Paul plays to the intellectual sensibilities of his learned listeners. After all, most scholars will at least concede that many things remain unknown; and the term used by Paul in Acts 17:23 is a form of the word *agnosticism*. As Cornelius Van Til put it, "Even among the cultured it was in good style to recognize the fact that there was more in heaven and on earth than they had yet dreamed of in their philosophy . . . they were perfectly willing therefore to leave open a place for the unknown."[1] Opening his message in this way was a genius stroke.

Can you imagine how different this story would read if Paul had chosen to employ an iconoclastic strategy in Athens rather than an integrative one? If he had taken a sledgehammer to the altars, or led a boycott against the festivals, or plastered a slogan "against the Athenian way" on billboards entering the city, it certainly would have made his message intelligible. But it also might have done great harm to the gospel. Bombastic strategies may rid the world of its pagan or religious external symbols—but whenever Christians adopt such strategies, they fail to win the minds and hearts of those who live and walk among the idols.

Yes, many today will be called upon to preach in great cities, and such preachers would do well to adopt the interpersonal and integrative strategies that have helped win cities in the past.

The Citizen and His Culture

It is one thing to know where our audience can be found. It is quite another to know who our audience is and what customs define it. The world today is filled with people who do not know the Bible, and none of us should ever be satisfied to preach without scores of them in attendance. Gospel preachers make it a point to have listeners from among those who are *in* the world, for non-Christians are a pivotal audience for the Word. If we want our messages to reach today's audience, we need to give rightful attention to its cultural context. We will need to be able to speak the culture's language. Thankfully, there are more than enough books and articles that address this need. There isn't much more that I could add, though I would offer the caution that good biblical expositors should know the limits of this kind of preparation. Just because contextualization is done well, it does not necessarily mean that our preaching will be readily understood, let alone that we will necessarily transform culture.

Again, we need look no further than Paul's Athenian discourse in Acts 17:16–34 to see that this is the case. While Paul did his best to contextualize his message to his audience (as should we), Luke observes that this good and necessary work had limited effect. One Athenian reacted to Paul's gospel preaching with, "What does this babbler wish to say?" (17:18). The word translated as *babbler* means *seed picker* or *scavenger*, as if Paul is grabbing one idea from here and another from over there and the results are incoherent. This is the kind of reaction that someone who blindly adheres to contextualization claims to overcome.

Don't let Luke's record be lost on you: Paul, who gives us the model of contextualization, was mocked by some for preaching a message that had no unifying center and, therefore, no ability to sway public opinion (see Acts 17:32). Another reaction to Paul's message was: "'He seems to be a preacher of foreign divinities' because he was preaching Jesus and the resurrection" (v. 18). The phrase "foreign divinities" suggests that part of the Athenian problem had to do with understanding Paul's meaning. In essence, when the Athenians first heard the gospel, they thought it strange, unfamiliar, and outside their present pantheon.

My point in drawing attention to these two reactions to Paul is to say, yes, give yourself to the work of understanding today's citizen and his culture, but don't think that good biblical expositors will always prove comprehensible or compelling to people today.

Finally, I am reminded not only of our need for prayer, but for the attending power of the Holy Spirit in all our preaching. This indeed is our greatest need. Preachers must understand the true source of power. The role that the Holy Spirit plays in birthing churches through God's Word and in challenging the supremacy of all citizens and cultures is indispensable. True life and true change in our hearers does not come from our ingenuity, but from the Word of the Spirit (John 6:63), set forth in plain speech, by a preacher who is looking to God.

By conviction then, may we who aspire to expound God's Word abandon all pretense and show—all conventions in preaching—anything that betrays a belief that the power rests somehow in us. Preaching demands humility. We must be done with undue interest in artistry or form. We disown fame, acclaim, and the trappings of avarice:

> For our appeal does not spring from error or impurity or any attempt to deceive, but just as we have been approved by God to be entrusted with the gospel, so we speak, not to please man, but to please God who tests our hearts. For we never come with words of flattery, as you know, nor with a pretext for greed—God is witness. Nor did we seek glory from people, whether from you or from others. (1 Thess. 2:3–6)

2. THE ARRANGEMENT OF YOUR MATERIAL

Each week the preacher faces a similar challenge: How should I arrange the material I intend to preach? What organization will I bring to it? These questions are good and worthwhile.

Once you have exegeted and theologically reflected on the text, you will have a storehouse of rich and profitable things to say, and you are quite right to want to reward your listeners with the fruit of your labor. Given that, what should govern us in the arrangement of the material? And what positive role will contextualization have to play? I believe you need to prepare along two lines:

The Need for Clarity
The Advantages of Textual Conformity

The first leans heavily on contextualization, while the second holds firmly to the biblical text.

The Need for Clarity

A couple of years ago, I sat with Dick Lucas in his living room in London, England. Our conversation turned naturally to what God was doing in the church. Both of us were hopeful and excited about the promise we saw in the coming generation of preachers. In the middle of this upbeat exchange, he interjected, "Yes, but we must remind them that our preaching can never be too simple." After preaching for nearly fifty years to businesspeople who work in London's financial district, Lucas had learned something really important: the great ones are the clear ones. Preachers cannot be too simple. *We need clarity*.

I have noticed the same thing. While we have a generation of eager and emerging preachers dotting the landscape today, many still need to learn the art of arranging their material in ways that are clear and concise. This is where contextualization has a wonderful role to play.

Expository preachers recognize that the people they address week in and week out are not, generally speaking, as excited as they are about all the exegetical nuances and textual puzzles that were mastered during the week. One of my own godly businessmen put it to me this way: "Dave, what is the takeaway this week? Don't talk at me for the better part of thirty minutes without making things clear. I need simple hangers and direct speech."

A fruitful preacher knows the trenches in which his people live and work. He knows their needs and speaks their language. He is comfortable preaching to the believing and nonbelieving person alike, even if a good portion of his own week was spent alone in the study of the church manse.

As you begin the contextual work of arranging your material, do the legwork of making sure that your preaching is clear. Pay close attention to the words you use and the manner in which you make points. Be content if the glories of Christ are made clear only for those who come to hear. As Paul encouraged, "Continue steadfastly in prayer. . . . Pray also for us . . . that I may make it *clear*, which is how I ought to speak" (Col. 4:2–4).

Two practical steps can help with clarity:

State the Text's Theme
Articulate the Author's Aim

Biblical expositors don't step into the pulpit to preach without first being able to articulate the *theme* of their text in one coherent sentence. The theme is the big idea or dominant issue of the text. It is the point that the author is making. For instance, I recently began a message on James 4:1–12 by simply stating, "The issue James would like us to consider together for the next thirty minutes is our words, their ability to rupture relationships within the church, the source of that power, and what can be done about it." Whether you say it as bluntly as I did, being able to put the author's primary teaching point before your congregation in one sentence will help you with simplicity and clarity, two hallmarks of good style.

A second practical step a biblical expositor can use to aid clarity is to state in a single sentence the biblical author's *aim* for his audience from the text. The aim is what the author wants his audience to do or how he wants them to think differently—the action or the reaction—as a result of his theme. Even if you don't put it in a single sentence in your sermon, you should have it worked out before stepping into the pulpit. You should be able to answer the question, what does the author want from his readers?

Being able to state the author's aim has immense benefits—not the least of which is that it simplifies your task in contextualization. Biblical expositors are not pining away in their studies searching for ways to bring relevancy to their message. They don't need to. The Bible *is* relevant. Rather, they draw out the implications and applications that are already there in the text in ways that make sense for the culture the church is embedded in. In this way, the text of Scripture and the task of contextualization work hand in hand. They are partners in the work of preaching. And when they are used in this way, not only is the preacher more likely to be faithful and fruitful, but his sermons will become clearer and easier to follow.

The Advantages of Textual Conformity

This same dynamic relationship between text and contextualization should occur when biblical expositors turn to outlining their messages. Contextualization is handmaiden to text. The organization of your sermons should ordinarily follow the organization of the biblical text. Your preaching outline emerges from your exegetical and biblical and theological work. In fact, it becomes the contextualized mirror image of them.

This principle is the natural outworking of what exposition means. We don't superimpose our outline over the text. Rather, we bring out of the text what the Holy Spirit already put in. And that is best done in the manner in which he put it together. Remember, Charles Simeon was aiming at this when he said: "My endeavor is to bring out of Scripture what is there, and not to thrust in what I think might be there. I have a great jealousy on this head never to speak more or less than I believe to be the mind of the Spirit in the passage I am expounding."[2]

I have defined biblical exposition as empowered preaching that rightly submits the shape and emphasis of the sermon to the shape and emphasis of a biblical text. Perhaps it might be helpful to see what I intend by each of the key words in my definition. By *shape and emphasis* I mean that every natural preaching unit in the Bible comes ready-made with a Spirit-intended organization and emphasis. The job of the preacher is to find it. That is best done through the disciplined work of exegesis and theological reflection. Once that shape and emphasis are clearly apprehended, the preacher is ready to think about sermon construction.

What sets the construction of an exposition apart from other kinds of Bible talks is this: the preacher *rightly submits* the arrangement of the material to the shape and emphasis of the text. We don't impose some other outline upon it. And further, we don't interpose material not included in it. These two concerns are addressed in the phrase *rightly submits*. We need preachers who submit themselves to the right retelling of the good news.

Too many of us are loose in the cage. Our outlines are not fit. We construct messages that mirror something other than the text. They possess a different shape. This is an indication that we are not nearly disciplined enough in this part of our preparation. We don't submit the outline and emphasis of our talks to the text. Instead, we have the text conform to whatever shape and emphasis suits our fancy that particular week. As a result, we fall short of exposition, and cheat our people out of hearing God's voice. They are left with only our deficient voices instead. So, I would encourage you to work toward producing messages from the Bible that are committed to textual conformity. After all, this is biblical exposition, and as the subtitle of this little book states, this is *how we speak God's Word today*.

Having looked at the beneficial role contextualization can play in matters of *audience* and *arrangement,* we are ready to see how it assists you in *the application of your message.*

3. THE APPLICATION OF YOUR MESSAGE

When it comes to application, the first thing to be said is that biblical expositors aim for a *change of heart*. We are not merely looking to apply God's truths to the minds of our listeners, as important as that work is. Nor are we content merely to put their hands and feet to work, as necessary as Christian service may be. Rather, we pursue the hearts of our listeners. Our preaching should never settle for applications that merely compartmentalize how one thinks or what one does. Rather, as biblical expositors, our goal is to completely capture the will and the affections of our listeners for God. The heart is the seat of power. And the heart is the agent of change.

A full-orbed heart application partners with contextualization in at least four ways. It will:

Heart Repentance

Let's return again to Paul's sermon at Athens. There, he preached for *heart repentance*. He called for the citizens of Athens to "repent" (Acts 17:30) and not remain in "the times of ignorance." Paul wanted nothing less from the Athenians than a complete turning of the mind, heart, and will.

During sermon preparation, a preacher should ask himself a number of questions when he thinks through applying the text: Am I preaching for an internal change of heart? Am I reticent to call for repentance? Is my message more than merely intellectual?

Remember, the goal of contextualization is not to help the message of the gospel become one more interesting fact. Rather, we set out to win the hearts of our listeners to the full praise that Christ deserves. And for this exalted work to occur, it will take the Spirit of God to apply the Word of God to the people of God. Who can change the human heart but God alone (a point ironically understood by Jesus's enemies; see Mark 2:7)?

Heart Prayer

Since the goal of sermon application is completely repentant hearts, and since only God can bring about this goal, we must approach the application portion of our preparation on our knees. We must be familiar with heart prayer.

Luke 11:1–13 encourages us to this end. The disciples came to Jesus wanting to learn how to pray, just as John had taught his disciples. In response, Jesus provided them with a pattern for praying (Luke 11:1–4). Then he spoke a parable to encourage them in the work of prayer by contrasting God as Father with a close friend. A friend who is awoken in the middle of the night may not offer assistance. Friendship has its limits! But God as Father is not like such a friend. He stands ready to help us. Ask, and you will receive. Knock, and he will open. And what exactly does God promise to give us? "The heavenly Father [will] give the Holy Spirit to those who ask him!" (11:13). Not even John the Baptist's disciples, who had been taught to pray, knew about the Holy Spirit (Acts 19:1–2). But, thank God, we are aware. And God promises to give him to us!

Heart Awareness

Just as we must open up our hearts to God for the souls of our people, so too we should know the hearts of our people. At its best, contextualization helps us to see what controls the hearts of those around us. Simply put, if the application of our message serves to capture the hearts of our people for God, we need to possess a heart awareness of our people. We must perceive, by careful watching, their internally held values and commitments, especially those things that keep them from living lives that are rightly ordered in worship and obedience to Christ.

The writings of Augustine and the Epistles of Paul (as well as the writings about his preaching in Acts) contain indispensable material for preachers to meditate on in the work of contextualization. In fact, the writings of these two men alone could suffice in serving the expositor's need. It is ludicrous to think that merely referencing *The Economist* or *The New York Times* can get the job done. This kind of writing, more often than not, fails to get beyond *what* is going on in the world. The matter of *why* men do what they do is the essential part. And uncovering that will always be a matter of the *heart!* No one exemplifies this facility better than Augustine and Paul. They show you *how* you can make use of *The Economist* and *Times*.

Fortunately, what Augustine and Paul demonstrate can be acquired. For example, Princeton historian Peter Brown puts exactly this kind of heart awareness on display through his own research and reading on ancient Rome. He writes of the *amor civicus* of the citizens of Rome, their "love for the city and its citizens." He continues:

> A rich person who showed this love was acclaimed as an *amator patriae*—a lover of his or her hometown. It was the most honorable love that a wealthy person could show. *Amor civicus* was written all over the temples, the forums and public buildings, the arches, the colonnades, and the vast places of public entertainment—the theaters, the amphitheaters, and the stadium-like circuses—which still amaze the tourist to any Roman site in almost any region of western Europe and north Africa.[3]

Brown describes the people of Rome as having "landscapes of the heart." He describes them as "lovers of homeland" and "lovers whose heart was Rome."[4] Were Brown actually preaching to the people of Rome, this is exactly the sort of knowledge that could be put to excellent use in sermon application. Like ancient Rome, our cities are places where worldviews collide. Yet the hearts of men and women are on display. And you and I must learn the listening skills that Peter Brown demonstrates so well.

To apply God's Word today with penetrating insight, it helps to know what our citizenry love, cherish, and value. Have you done that? Do you possess a heart awareness of people in your context?

The Heart of the Biblical Text

While every preacher needs heart awareness, it is wrong to think that's all a preacher needs to make good gospel applications. Remember, a healthy gospel ministry is always contextually informed—but textually driven.

Some preachers become so audience-driven, so contextually focused, that when it comes time to prepare sermon applications, they forget their text! I have actually heard preachers describe their application preparation time this way: they sit in their study with their eyes closed, heads back, faces tilted toward the ceiling. They whisper things to themselves like, "Now, I know that Bobby will be there, and he is thirteen years old and facing identity issues. . . . How can I apply this to his heart? And Billy-Sue will be there, bless her heart, and she is battling depression . . ."

This highly contextualized strategy does have a place, but it must not be primary. The preacher can better serve his people with his eyes open and his face planted *in the text*. The key to remember is this: applications for your message are always connected to *the heart of the biblical text*. To find them, you need to ask better questions—not questions about your people, but questions of the text.

A question I always ask of my text is, what intention does the biblical author have for his readers? This is, by far, the best place to start. It aligns my thoughts with the aim of the author. Articulating the intention of the text puts us further down the road to finding the text's implications or applications for our hearers. Sometimes we find the author's intention in an explicit declaration. In these cases, he is handing us our application. For instance, in the account of David and Goliath, we read this:

> This day the LORD will deliver you into my hand, and I will strike you down and cut off your head. And I will give the dead bodies of the host of the Philistines this day to the birds of the air and to the wild beasts of the earth, that all the earth may know that there is a God in Israel, and that all this assembly may know that the LORD saves not with sword and spear. For the battle is the LORD's, and he will give you into our hand. (1 Sam. 17:46–47)

Here the text gives us the point of the story: the battle serves an evangelistic purpose ("that all the earth may know that there is a God in Israel") and an edification purpose, teaching God's people to trust in him ("the LORD saves not with sword and spear. For the battle is the LORD's.").

A second helpful question to ask of the text is, how are the characters in this text responding to God's truth, or God's Anointed? Sometimes—though not always—characters become a foil for congregants. I once preached on a passage that shows a contrast between two kings—Saul and David (1 Samuel 22). It is a fascinating chapter, one that has two minor characters sharing the stage with the famous kings. The first is Doeg the Edomite, and he aligns himself with Saul. The second is Abiathar, who decides to follow David. Doeg and Abiathar become useful characters for sermon application. Will we follow God's Anointed, even though he appears weak and is on the run? Or, will we be like Doeg, and follow the earthly king whose power and benefits will ultimately fail?

A third helpful question is, is this application the primary application of this text or merely a possible one? You should not in general grab a secondary or tertiary application before making sure that you have driven home that which is primary. You want your primary aim to match the Holy Spirit's primary aim with a text. Think of this question along the lines of a ladder in which each application gets more and more abstract. The further away a rung is on the ladder, the more foolish you are to reach for it. It is simply too far removed, and you are better off holding onto something closer, stronger, clearer, and primary.

On those occasions when I do want to apply my text in multiple ways, I always lead with the primary one. The further away I get, I tell my congregation that what I'm saying is more of a stretch. Think back to the discussion of 1 Samuel 2 in chapter 1. Some of the applications were about parenting. But as we studied the text, we saw that such applications are secondary or even tertiary.

Another helpful question that checks my applications

against the restraints of the text is, does this application undermine my text? Just because an application is possible doesn't mean that the author had it in mind. A related question is, does my application contradict other biblical texts? If it does, I don't use it. Think about the time David lied to the priest Ahimelech in order to get food and arms (1 Samuel 21). You might use this text to argue for "holy deception" in the service of God, but you are going to have problems when you arrive at Colossians 3:9–10. This last question helps to keep you from inadvertently pitting Scripture against Scripture.

A final check on my work is to ask a question that points me back to the heart of the Bible itself. Is the application I am making grounded in the gospel, or am I in danger of simply placing more commands on my people? When preaching James 3:1–12, for example, it would be very easy to say, "Get control of your tongue." But it is moralism if we just leave it at that. The point of the chapter is that controlling our tongues is impossible. We need grace. James goes on to make this point in verses 13–18. We look for wisdom "from above."

ONE FINAL WORD

To best make an impact today, preachers must partner contextualization with the biblical text. Not only that, but we have benefited from each of them in ways that help us with the makeup of our *audience*, the *arrangement* of our material, and the *application* of our message.

One final word, and we are done. The best biblical expositors, while immensely concerned with *today*, nevertheless do all their sermon work (whether it be exegesis, theological reflection, or contextualization) in light of *the day*—that day when Jesus returns, when all things will be made known, including the motivations of the preacher's heart. May your knowledge of that day help you to remain prayerful and faithful, and to leave the abundance of fruit in the hands of God.

CONCLUSION

Dry Bones

Upon ordination, Charles Simeon preached his first sermon on Trinity Sunday while filling in for a pastor on vacation. At the time, Simeon was only twenty-two. Decades later, he would reflect on his first efforts in the pulpit. He wrote:

> Being now acquainted with Mr. Atkinson, I undertook the care of his church during the long vacation; and I have reason to hope that some good was done there. In the space of a month or six weeks the church became quite crowded; the Lord's Table was attended by three times the usual number of communicants, and a considerable stir was made among the dry bones.[1]

As a preacher, I love everything about Simeon's brief description of his first sermons: from the ordinary way he got started—filling the pulpit for a man on vacation—to his simple expression of hope for being useful. What a wonderful beginning! I even suppose that God caused those early messages to be especially fruitful as a special gift, meant to help him later in the ministry. After all, he would soon encounter many trials in Cambridge. Perhaps most of all, I love the pathos in how he viewed the impact of the preached Word: "a considerable stir was made among the dry bones."

I am firmly convinced that what happened in Simeon's day, by God's grace, can happen again. And perhaps it will begin with you! In writing this brief book on preaching, I have kept this twenty-two-year-old close in my mind. So whether you are twenty-two or eighty-two, or somewhere in between, I pray that God will use your ministry in ways that give us all "hope that some good was done."

APPENDIX

Questions Preachers Ask

Here are some diagnostic questions you can use to guide you in your sermon preparation from beginning to end.

EXEGESIS

Have I prayed for God's help as I begin my work?

Structure

How has the author organized this text? It will be helpful if you can clearly indicate the verse breaks for each part of the structure.

General: Is there a repeated word, phrase, or idea in the text?

Narrative: How is the text divided into scenes? Is it organized around geography or shifts in characters? What is the plot? (What is the conflict, or what is providing dramatic tension? What is the climax or turning point? Is the tension resolved? If so, how?)

Discourse: How does the grammar or logic of the passage show the flow of ideas?

Poetry: How does the tone or subject of this poem shift?

What does the organization reveal about the author's intended emphasis?

Context

How does the immediate literary context—the passages on both sides of the text—inform the meaning of the text? Why is this passage here in this place?

What was the historical situation faced by the first audience or, depending on genre, the first readers?

How does the passage fit within a larger section?

Melodic Line

What is the essence of this book?

How is the passage informing and informed by the melodic line?

What is the theme of the text?

THEOLOGICAL REFLECTION

How does the text anticipate or relate to the gospel?

How does biblical theology help me see the gospel in the text? How is the author using *prophetic fulfillment*, *historical trajectory*, *themes*, or *analogies*?

How does systematic theology help me see the gospel in the text? Is it holding me in the faith, helping me connect to the gospel, or honing my ability to speak to non-Christians?

CONTEXTUALIZATION AND TODAY

Audience

Do I know the people who will be hearing this sermon? Have I pledged myself in love to them? Have I been in prayer for them throughout my preparation?

Arrangement

What shape and emphasis will I bring to my sermon? Does that shape and emphasis reflect the structure and emphasis of the text?

Application

Am I preaching for an internal change of heart, both in my life and the lives of my listeners? Am I doing so in ways that rightly humble the listener, exalt the Savior, and promote holiness in the lives of those present?

What aim or intention does the biblical author have for his readers?

Narrative: How are the characters in the text responding to God's truth, or to God's Anointed?

Discourse/poetry: How does the author want his readers to respond?

Does my application follow from the author's aim?

Is my application the primary application of the text, or merely a possible one?

Does my application undermine the text? Does it contradict other biblical texts?

Is the application I am making grounded in the gospel, or am I in danger of simply placing more commands on my people?

Am I leaning on the text to say what I want to say? Or am I bringing out of Scripture only what is there?

SPECIAL THANKS

Two pastors modeled expositional preaching for me: Kent Hughes and Dick Lucas. These men not only patterned their week around the explication of God's Word, but they also found time to invest in me as well. And for that, I thank them. They remain dear friends, and I am sure that these pages are better because of them.

In addition, I want to express appreciation to the two pastors with whom I work most closely, Jon Dennis and Arthur Jackson. Your many years of faithful ministry encourage me. I am indebted to Holy Trinity Church, Hyde Park, Chicago. For fifteen years now you have gladly received God's Word from me. And more than that, together, week by week, we have pledged our hearts to one another through the word of Christ. How thankful I am for that, as well as for how happy God has made us under Christ's rule.

Also, I am grateful for the friendship of Mark Dever and Jonathan Leeman. It is only through their kind invitation and continued insistence that these ideas be put to paper that time was made for writing. Gentlemen, thanks for the chance you have given me to stand with you in this work. Additionally, the editorial work of Tara Davis at Crossway has made the text of this book stronger. Thank you.

Closer to home again, I am incredibly thankful to God for

Robert Kinney, friend in the cause of Christ. Thanks, as always, for making a manuscript better, and even more so, for sharing the responsibilities of leading the Charles Simeon Trust with me.

Finally, to Lisa, for your lifelong bands of love, graciously reserved for me alone for three decades now, I thank you. I especially love the ever-enlarging place you make in your heart for God's Word.

NOTES

Introduction: Old Bones

1. For the details surrounding the funeral and burial place of Charles Simeon, I am indebted to William Carus. William Carus, *Memoirs of the Life of the Rev. Charles Simeon* (London: Hatchard and Son, 1847), 582–83.

2. Handley Carr Glyn Moule, *Charles Simeon* (London: Methuen & Co., 1892), 97.

3. Charles Simeon, *Horae Homileticae* (Grand Rapids, MI: Zondervan, 1847), xxi.

Chapter 1: Contextualization

1. Peter Brown, *Through the Eye of a Needle* (Princeton, NJ: Princeton University Press, 2012), 54.

2. This line drawing, which develops throughout the book, is my own take on a graphic done some time ago by Edmund Clowney in *Preaching Christ in All of Scripture* (Wheaton, IL: Crossway, 2003), 32. I work off it in the way church musicians take an old hymn and write a new arrangement of music for it.

3. Bernard Denvir, *The Thames and Hudson Encyclopaedia of Impressionism* (London: Thames and Hudson, 1990).

4. The origin of the Andrew Lang story and quote is uncertain, though it has been widely cited in quotation collections such as Elizabeth M. Knowles, *The Oxford Dictionary of Quotations*, 7th ed. (Oxford: Oxford University Press, 2009), 478:12.

5. Handley Carr Glyn Moule, *Charles Simeon* (London: Methuen & Co., 1892), 97.

Chapter 2: Exegesis

1. How you balance the historical and literary context and what questions you ask of a text will depend, in part, on the book you are preaching. In an epistle, for example, you want to know about the historical situation of the church or individual to whom the letter was written. But you will not necessarily want to read a Gospel this same way. If the Gospels were meant to be distributed throughout the world, then the first historical audience to whom each Evangelist was writing is less important than the literary context of how the Evangelist put together his Gospel. On the audience of the Gospels, see Richard Bauckham, ed., *The Gospels for All Christians* (Grand Rapids, MI: Eerdmans, 1998).

2. Most epistles include purpose statements as a matter of form. Luke 1:1–4 and John 20:30–31 also serve as helpful examples of purpose statements.

3. Mortimer Adler and Charles Van Doren, *How to Read a Book: The Classic Guide to Intelligent Reading* (New York: Touchstone, 1940), 75.

Chapter 3: Theological Reflection

1. Charles Haddon Spurgeon, "Christ Precious to Believers" (sermon, Music Hall, Royal Surrey Gardens, March 13, 1859), http://www.spurgeon.org/sermons/0242.php

2. James Barr, *The Concept of Biblical Theology: An Old Testament Perspective* (London: SCM Press, 1999), 253–54.

3. Sidney Greidanus, *Preaching Christ from the Old Testament: A Contemporary Hermeneutical Method* (Grand Rapids, MI: Eerdmans, 1999), 234–40.

4. G. K. Beale, *Handbook on the New Testament Use of the Old Testament: Exegesis and Interpretation* (Grand Rapids, MI: Baker Academic, 2012), 14.

5. D. A. Carson, "Unity and Diversity in the New Testament: the Possibility of Systematic Theology," in *Scripture and Truth,* ed. D. A. Carson and John D. Woodbridge (Grand Rapids, MI: Baker, 1983), 69–70.

6. These two quotations come from the notes of A. W. Brown's

reflections on his times with Charles Simeon as part of Simeon's "conversation parties with the students of Cambridge." Abner William Brown, *Recollections of the Conversation Parties of the Rev. Charles Simeon, M.A: Senior Fellow of King's College, and Perpetual Curate of Trinity Church, Cambridge* (London: Hamilton, Adams, & Co, 1863), 269.

Chapter 4: Today

1. Cornelius Van Til, *Paul at Athens* (Phillipsburg, NJ: P&R, 1978), 6.

2. Handley Carr Glyn Moule, *Charles Simeon* (London: Methuen & Co., 1892), 97.

3. Peter Brown, *Through the Eye of a Needle* (Princeton: Princeton University Press, 2012), 64.

4. Ibid., 96–101.

Conclusion: Dry Bones

1. William Carus, *Memoirs of the Life of the Rev. Charles Simeon* (London: Hatchard and Son, 1847), 24.

GENERAL INDEX

SCRIPTURE INDEX

THE CHARLES SIMEON TRUST

David Helm is the chairman of the Charles Simeon Trust, an organization that seeks to increase your confidence and ability in handling God's Word. We do this in two important ways:

WORKSHOPS ON BIBLICAL EXPOSITION
A workshop consists of three parts: *principles* (simple instructional sessions on interpreting and teaching or preaching from the Bible), *preaching* (model expositions), and *practice* (interactive small groups on pre-assigned texts in order to improve skills). The workshops occur in more than 30 locations throughout the United States and around the world each year.

THE SIMEON COURSE ON BIBLICAL EXPOSITION
This course is an online training platform singularly focused on the practice of preaching and teaching of God's Word. Using web delivery and an HD video library of some of the best expositors and instructors in the world, we help our participants sharpen their skills. Any of our three courses can be taken for graduate credit: *Preaching and Literary Genre* (30 lessons), *Preaching and Biblical Theology* (15 lessons), and *Preaching and Systematic Theology* (15 lessons).

For more information, visit us at
www.simeontrust.org

9MARKS: BUILDING HEALTHY CHURCHES SERIES

Based on Mark Dever's best-selling book *Nine Marks of a Healthy Church*, each book in this series helps readers grasp basic biblical commands regarding the local church.

TITLES INCLUDE:

Biblical Theology	Conversion	The Gospel
Church Discipline	Discipling	Missions
Church Elders	Evangelism	Sound Doctrine
Church Membership	Expositional Preaching	

For more information, visit crossway.org.
For translated versions of these and other 9Marks books, visit 9Marks.org/bookstore/translations.

IX 9Marks

Building Healthy Churches

9Marks exists to equip church leaders with a biblical vision and practical resources for displaying God's glory to the nations through healthy churches.

To that end, we want to see churches characterized by these nine marks of health:

1   Expositional Preaching
2   Biblical Theology
3   A Biblical Understanding of the Gospel
4   A Biblical Understanding of Conversion
5   A Biblical Understanding of Evangelism
6   Biblical Church Membership
7   Biblical Church Discipline
8   Biblical Discipleship
9   Biblical Church Leadership

Find all our Crossway titles
and other resources at
www.9Marks.org